Mastering the Job Interview

Lavie Margolin

H. Delilah Business & Career Press

ISBN: 0692835555
ISBN-13: 978-0692835555

To the Dreamers.

CONTENTS

1 HOW TO PREPARE FOR YOUR JOB INTERVIEW

The phone rings and you are invited in for a job interview. You have worked so hard to get to this point: finding the right people to network with, digging for job listings and sharpening your resume and cover letter. Perhaps you feel that your friendly demeanor and history of professional accomplishment will carry you the rest of the way? Hardly. The interview is your opportunity to prove to the company that you should be given a chance and you cannot just wing it. By learning the right techniques to succeed in a job interview, you will stand out and increase your chances for getting the job.

Many of us dismiss our ability to have a good interview by feeling that we are just not good in that type of situation and will never get better. Everyone struggles with interviewing at first but you have to learn from every situation.

If you had an interview and it was not successful, what do you feel can be improved for next time? Were there certain questions that stumped you? Did you not know what to ask when prompted if you had any questions? Did you become confused on how to properly close the interview?

Read up on how to best answer certain types of interview questions. Practice in front of a mirror, with a friend, with a family member, with a professional in the field or with a Career Coach. The more you practice, the more comfortable you will be in the actual interview situation.

Prepare: Think of the type of questions you would like to ask before the interview so you are not stumped when the situation actually presents itself. Come back stronger for each interview and it will become easier and easier for the interviewer to see you in the job.

RESEARCH

Preparing for a job interview does not start with practicing interview questions, it begins by learning about the company. You can be the most qualified candidate in the world but if you do not demonstrate a good understanding of the company and industry, you will be unlikely to get the job.

Start your research by reading over the job description. Is there a certain division that is referenced at the company? If you know where to focus your efforts, it will save you time as you conduct detailed research. A multi-national conglomerate may have 20 divisions in 6 regions. You do not need to know more than the basics about the organization in general but you should have a good understanding of the division's areas of focus.

Start your research on the company website. Read the general mission statement, explore the organization's history and review the various divisions at the company. Find the sub site for your division. Examine this area closely and make notes for yourself.

Google the company name + the division you will be interviewing for. See what articles you can find.

Independently written stories will provide you with a more neutral look into the company as compared to information that has been processed via the corporate bullhorn on the company website.

Your review of the company website will invariably lead you to LinkedIn.com. You will be able to examine the profiles of many professionals in your area of interest, learn more about what they do day to day as well as any personal or divisional accomplishments that are listed. You will likely even be able to find your interviewer's information.

LinkedIn is great as a research tool but you have to be careful. If many employees in the division notice that you are looking at their profiles, it could get awkward. You want to demonstrate that you are doing your research but not necessarily let everyone know that you are looking at their profiles. Consider using LinkedIn in more of a stealth manner. You can switch your settings so that you will appear anonymously when people on LinkedIn check who has viewed their profiles. Alternatively, you can sign out of LinkedIn and use keyword searching on Google to find the LinkedIn profiles that you are looking for. Please note that if you are not signed in (or if you do not have an account at all), you will not be able to see as much information.

After conducting your research, you should prepare a few questions that you can ask during the interview. These questions should play off the research that you conducted and demonstrate your strong knowledge of the company and division:

- With competitor X now entering the same international markets, how might it change your client centered approach?

- Given the general economic downturn in Brazil, will you be looking to other international markets or continue to focus on the Brazilian market?

- How do you feel the increased reliance on technology and cloud based computing changes the strategy for selling computer security systems?

As shown in the examples above, you are not asking generic questions. You are demonstrating that you have learned enough about the industry, competitors, economic conditions and technology to ask the questions that dig a little deeper. These types of questions help to put you closer to the position of colleagues talking, instead of a strictly interviewer-interviewee relationship.

INTERVIEW ATTIRE

To make the right impression during an interview, it is not just what you say but how you are dressed. The natural inclination for job seekers is to dress as formally as possible. In many circumstances, this is the right way to go but it is not always the correct answer.

You want the company to envision you in the role for which you are interviewing. Part of building that perception on the interviewer's behalf is looking the part. Every company has its own culture. Some places of business are very buttoned up and require formal attire while other places are very casual in the dress code for employees. You are probably less likely to make the mistake of being too informal but you could make the mistake of being too formal as well. For example, let us consider a tech start up. It may be run by two 20 year olds who are less focused on formality and more on getting the job done. If you show up in a three-piece suit and company employees are wearing polo shirts and jeans, it could be awkward for you. It will be hard for the employer to imagine you in the role to which you aspire when you do not appear to be fitting in during the interview.

How can you know what is appropriate to wear for your upcoming interview? Generally speaking, there are certain industry standards that shouldn't be too hard to figure out. Within industries such as law, finance and accounting, there is an expectation of formality. In other industries, it can get a bit more complicated. Some advertising firms are more traditional and expect employees to wear button down suits and ties whereas others may expect dress shirts and khaki pants.

There are several ways for you to conduct your research to determine what the company culture is like when it comes to dress:

1. Look at the company website. What are employees wearing in their profile pictures or any additional pictures that you can find on the site?

2. Examine LinkedIn profiles of current employees to see how they are dressed.

3. Ask colleagues who can provide you with insight into the company culture. The person need not have worked for the company in order to understand the culture of the company. Your contact may have done business with the company or know people who work there.

4. Get connected to current employees or even former employees to learn. LinkedIn is a helpful tool to learn who you know that is connected with someone at your company of interest. Don't reach out cold (without an introduction) as

it could make for an awkward situation if you are reaching out to someone you do not know, just to find out what you should be wearing on an interview. The person that connects you could act as a buffer and explain your concerns in making the right impression by dressing correctly for the interview.

If you are still not confident of what to wear on a job interview, it is better to err on the side of caution. It is better to be overdressed as opposed to underdressed for an interview.

It is always interesting to look back on professional mistakes that we made along the way, especially those that seem so obvious in retrospect:

When I graduated from college with a degree in marketing, I applied to several advertising agencies, public relations firms and marketing companies. The process of securing initial interviews was no problem. The challenge was actually getting called back for the second round of interviews.

I had read that advertising professionals are more laid back in the office and do not wear a suit or a tie. To show that I could fit in, I went to every interview with just a button down shirt and slacks. I never wore a suit or a tie. It took me a while to realize that I had to dress more professionally in order to be taken seriously on an interview, no matter what the regular corporate culture.

Even though one may dress on the job a certain way, you have to dress one level above that for the interview to be taken seriously. Once I started dressing more professionally, I started getting called back for additional rounds of interviews. Eventually, I was able to use this early professional lesson for myself as a helpful anecdote in helping job seekers.

I don't have a passion for fashion but there is just something that feels great about wearing a nice new pair of shoes, slacks or sports jacket. Not too long ago, I was reminded of how clothing can change the outlook on how you feel. Let me take you back a little bit. During Hurricane Sandy, our home in Long Beach flooded. My work pants were in the washing machine and were ruined. I remembered the only pants that I had remaining were in a big plastic garbage bag- I was planning to give my heavily worn out pants away to those who were in need of clothing. I didn't realize that it would end up being me! Without being truly situated for months and lacking the time to go to the store or even to shop online, I made due as best as possible with what I had.

There was just something about wearing slacks that were frayed on the bottom and a tearing seam by the pants pocket that hurt my confidence when interacting with other professionals. When my wife came home with six pairs of new pants, it made me feel great. When interviewing for a job, our confidence is naturally shaky to begin with. If you are going on an interview and your pants are a bit worn or you are trying to hide the stain on your tie, it will distract from you being able to give the best interview possible.

Invest in new clothing when you are interviewing. Being able to break out a new pair of shoes, tie or sports coat, will increase your confidence and allow you to focus on the most important parts of your interview- the company and you.

GET RHYTHM

The top athletes in the world are always practicing their craft. A winning football team does not rely upon their athletic talents to carry the day, they expect to get better in practice and then apply those principles on the field. A rock band doesn't show up 5 minutes before they are set to perform. They practice the songs that they have already performed hundreds of times, they conduct a sound check and they loosen up their vocal cords in the back of the arena. When approaching a job interview, you must take a similar serious approach to your preparation.

Have you ever walked out of an interview feeling that you weren't at your best until you had answered a handful of questions? It takes time to find your rhythm during the actual interview. Consider getting yourself into the interviewing mindset days before the actual interview. You can put yourself into the right mindset by practicing for an interview in several different scenarios. By the time you reach the actual interview, you will be ready for almost anything that is asked.

As you read through this book, you will find 500 interview questions, with an explanation of the reason the question is being asked as well as a sample answer. Use this as your guide when preparing for an interview. You can ask yourself the question and then answer it. Try doing so out loud so you can hear yourself and even stand in front of a mirror, so that you can see yourself. If you can, record yourself so you can play it back to see where you can improve.

If you can find someone to ask the questions to you, it will allow you to get into a better rhythm. The person can go through several questions with you before you take a break;

similar to an actual job interview. You can review your answers together and receive feedback from the person who (mock) interviewed you in order for you to improve in the future. It may be a friend or relative that is helping you. Practice a session with one person and then try to find someone else later. This will help to break up the routine so that you do not get completely used to the interview style of the person that is interviewing you.

Ideally, you will practice with someone who can give you pointed feedback as to where you could improve. A family member or friend might have suggestions, but it wouldn't be as strong as someone with a solid understanding of the industry. This might include an experienced professional in this industry, a person who has conducted interviews before such as a recruiter or hiring manager or even a knowledgeable career counselor/coach.

UNDERSTANDING THE NEEDS OF THE INTERVIEWER

What do interviewers actually want to hear? This is a mystery that has befuddled many of us. The best way to understand what an interviewer wants is to put your self in his or her seat. No, don't take the seat of the interviewer when offered the chance to sit down! All kidding aside, if you were hiring, what type of answers would you want to hear? You would want the answers that gave you confidence that this candidate is the best fit for the position.

Bearing in mind that you should provide an answer that gives the interviewer confidence that you are the best fit for the job, you can answer any question thrown at you. Consider what the company is looking for and answer honestly within the context of that question.

For example, if you are asked what is your greatest strength, focus on a strength that this employer would value.

If you are asked to share your proudest accomplish, think about what accomplishment would be relevant to the position.

If you are told to explain where you see yourself in 5 years, consider the organization's hierarchy before you answer and provide a realistic answer.

The interviewer must be able to envision you in the role. The interview is not about you, it is about how you can honestly portray your relevant skills, experience and abilities for the position. No matter how off base the question seems, just consider what you can say that makes you a better candidate for the position and answer accordingly.

TAKE A PAR APPROACH TO ANSWERING QUESTIONS

Every job has its challenges. That is why companies have employees. The employees are responsible for identifying problems, taking action on the problem and providing results. If you can demonstrate a PAR approach on interviews, you will stand out as a strong candidate.

What is PAR?

P is for Problem. Identifying a particular problem.

A is for Action. What action did you take to resolve the problem?

R is for Result. What was the (hopefully positive) result of your action to resolve the problem?

When answering relevant questions, think of a PAR approach. Utilize stories and examples to prove your point.

If you are asked about challenging scenarios at work, with co-workers, clients or even machines: Explain the problem (or challenge), what you did to resolve the problem and what was the end result.

An interview is a chance to continue to sell an employer on your appropriateness for the job opening. Every answer that you give should make your candidacy stronger, including how you respond to "What is your greatest weakness?"

By saying, " I don't have any weaknesses", you are appearing too cocky and not answering the question.

By saying, "I work too hard. I'll often lose track of time when a deadline is approaching. I can get so engrossed in my work that I do not realize when it is after midnight!", you can come across as disingenuous or just providing a stock answer to get the question over with.

And you certainly don't want to provide a major weakness or flaw that you have that can keep you from actually getting the job. So what do you do? Take the P.A.R. approach.

Explain a challenge or problem that you may have had, what you went about doing to solve it and what the end result was. Try to keep it in the realm of the industry for which you are applying.

Here is an example: "I felt confident in my knowledge of most of Microsoft Office but I knew my Access skills needed some work. I have been working diligently to practice in the evenings, and watch online tutorials to learn all the unique features about the program. I now feel much more confident in my knowledge of the program and I continue to learn more every day."

An interviewer wants to get insight into how you will deal with challenges on the job. Show him/her how you approach a situation and can be successful no matter what the challenge.

KNOW THEIR ROLE

Interviewing with larger organization brings with it more complex layers to the interview process. Job seekers often make the mistake of thinking that the first person that interviews them is in the position to hire. The interview process often includes 3 or 4 rounds of interviews before a job offer is made. You should understand the role of each person interviewing you in order to tailor your answers to meet their expectations as well as use each round of interviews as a learning experience to improve for the next round of the interviewing process.

1. The Recruiter. Although seemingly in a role to recruit talent into an organization, they play a dual role of gatekeeper: keeping people out of the organization. Recruiters must sift through hundreds of resumes and find a handful of candidates to interview. The hiring manager doesn't have the time to look at every resume and needs the help of the recruiter to cut down the list of candidates.

* The role of the recruiter should not be confused with the role of the recruiter. Confused yet? There are internal recruiters and external recruiters. The internal recruiter works for the company and is part of the human resources team. The recruiter that is in an external role is offered referred to as a headhunter. This person works for a recruiting firm that is paid by the hiring organization on commission or is retained for a monthly fee to help in sourcing candidates.

The recruiter will ask you basic questions in order to determine your general qualifications for a position. The recruiter often does not have the technical knowledge to discuss your position in depth. He or she is looking for any signs of trouble or concern in your background such as an inconsistent work history of if you have ever been fired.

Keep your answers short and to the point. Address any potential concerns by bringing clarity to the situation and explaining what you might have learned. Avoid getting too technical in explaining your skills, experience and abilities.

2. The Hiring Manager. If all goes well with the recruiter, you will make the short list of those allowed to interview with the hiring manager. The manager will be the one directly overseeing your work.

The hiring manager is less concerned with asking abstract interview questions and is more focused on if you can do the work. He or she will want to get into the technical aspects of your expertise to determine if you know your stuff. Overall, the hiring manager wants to know if you have the expertise required and if you will be a good person to work with.

Prove to the hiring manager that you have the knowledge required to do the job. Utilize examples from your work history, education and training to prove your expertise. The PAR approach will be especially important here. You want the boss to envision how you have successfully approached and resolved problems in the past and how you can do it similarly in the future.

3. Potential future co-workers. The hiring manager often does not want to make a decision alone. The manager has been careful to build a team that can work well together and will be

cautious about disturbing the "eco system". The hiring manager's team may be asked to meet with you to get their feedback of what they think of you and how you might fit in.

The team wants to get to know you and if they can work with you. They may ask you about your relevant background and experience. This might be the least buttoned up part of the interviewing process as the team is really trying to get to know you as opposed to asking generic interview questions or trying to trip you up with confusing questions.

Be your professional self with the team but do not get too comfortable. Avoid using canned responses or seeming too buttoned up. Your goal is to establish a rapport with the team while maintaining your professionalism. Do not try too hard to be liked. If you are genuine and demonstrate that you are a serious professional and a good co-worker, you will stand out.

4. An Executive. A company executive may be required to give approval before the candidate is hired. The executive would like to make sure that you fit into the culture of the company and that you are the type of person who will represent the company well. The executive knows that you have been thoroughly screened to determine your technical capabilities for the job. He or she will focus on your organizational fit to determine his or her confidence in having you represent the company in this role. This interview will likely be brief as an executive's time is often limited and you have already been screened by many people.

Listen carefully to the questions that you are asked and succinctly respond with clarity as to why you are a good fit for the organization.

Some of the things that an executive would look for include:

-Are you the type of employee that the company would want representing the organization?

Are your values in line with company culture?

Are you passionate about the organization and not just the job?

What is important at this stage is to focus on your knowledge and interest in the company as well as the industry. Demonstrate that you have done your research and why you are interested in this company specifically. Do not get too technical, unless prompted to do so, regarding your ability to handle the minutia of the position. As the executive will have a general understanding of what you will be doing on a day to day basis on the job, he/she is likely to lose interest in discussing minutiae.

Allow the executive to take the lead during the interview. In a best case scenario, the executive interview is just a "rubber stamp". If all seems fine and there are no glaring question marks that come up at this stage, the executive will most likely approve the hire. Depending on your role, you may not be interacting with this executive on a day to day basis. By talking too much, you can sell yourself out of a job. Try to mirror the traits of other employees you have met at the company. Follow the lead of the interviewer and explain all of the positive things you have learned about the organization during the earlier stages of the process. You are almost at the finish line- keep pushing!

FROM INTERROGATION TO CONVERSATION

Are you a fan of police dramas or perhaps you have had an unfortunate run in with the law yourself? Do not worry as this is a judgment free zone. No matter how you acquired the information, you are probably familiar with the idea of a police interrogation: An officer or two peppering a suspect with questions as to his or her whereabouts. A job interview can often feel similar to an interrogation. We sit silently awaiting the next question, answer it and dread the question that is right behind it.

An interview does not have to be an interrogation. In fact, you are more likely to have greater success if you treat the interview like a professional conversation. How can you accomplish this? Ask questions. You have to wait your turn but you do not have to wait until the end of the interview to ask your questions. If you wait until the end of the interview to ask questions, your opportunity to make a good impression with the interviewer is already lost.

The best time to ask a question is after you answered a question. Provide a question that relates to your answer and the last question asked of you. Below are two examples:

A. Once you have answered what your two greatest strengths are, inquire as to what are some other strengths it would be helpful for an employee to have for the position.

B. Once you have discussed what your greatest accomplishment is, inquire as to what are some of the goals an employee in the open position would be expected to meet.

Pay attention to the social cues of the interviewer. If he or she does not seem to appreciate your questions, table them to the end. If your questions seem to be well received and you seem to be building a rapport with your interviewer, continue on. Don't feel that you need to produce a follow up question after every question that you answer. Let things flow and provide an occasional question.

During an interview, we are peppered with question after question. As the interview is coming to a close, we will be asked if we have any questions for the interviewer. This is often a wasted moment by the interviewee as they see this as their time to ask whatever they want and don't use it as an opportunity to continue to sell their fit for the job.

How many other candidates are interviewing for the position?

It doesn't matter how many other candidates are interviewing for the position. This shouldn't concern you at all. Are you hoping that you happen to be the most qualified person that interviews or do you want to demonstrate that you are the most qualified? Asking this question shows a lack of confidence to the interviewer. It doesn't matter if it is 3 people interviewing for the job or 110. You just have to put yourself in the best position to get the job.

Here are some other bad questions:

2. What is the salary?

Now is not the time. If you wait until you receive an offer, you will be in the best position to negotiate.

3. What are the hours for the position?

It makes you seem too "clock focused" and not dedicated to the job. Certainly ask before you accept an offer but not during an early interview.

4. Why is this position vacant?

Why does that matter? The interviewer might not want to discuss why someone was hired or quit the job. If the last person in this role got promoted, the interviewer will bring that up at some point.

5. Can you tell me more about the company?

You should have done your research already. Don't ask for general information on the company unless you are meeting with a (outside) recruiter or headhunter.

THE INTERVIEWING PITFALL TO AVOID

Interviewers are people too. Doing the same thing over and over again isn't usually too exciting. It can get boring spending several days interviewing candidates for a role. When something is unique on a resume, it is likely to elicit a topic of discussion during the interview. Perhaps you were in a one-hit wonder band in the seventies or played professional rugby?

The interviewer may want to ask you about your unique talent or interests and you can have a great conversation sharing your mutual interest in sports, your ability to play the guitar or passion for baseball card collecting.

You walk out the door feeling great because the interviewer will remember you. The interviewer liked you and now you are likely to get the job, right? Well, not so fast.

Will the interviewer remember you as a good person to hang out with and relax or will he/she remember you as a great candidate for the job?

The opportunity to sell yourself for the job is very limited. If you didn't take the opportunity to sell your skills, qualifications and abilities for a job, you didn't put yourself in the best position to succeed.

Wherever possible, refocus the interview on your

qualifications for the job vacancy at hand. How can you do that? Keep answers to unrelated (but interesting) questions short and sweet.

The interviewer should remember you as a great fit for the job and not just a cool person!

AVOID BEING TOO AGGRESSIVE

When I am on an interview, I try to mirror the interviewer. If she is very animated, I try to be animated. If he is more reserved, I try to be more reserved. You want to connect with the person and be able to build a professional rapport.

Similar to every aspect of the job search (and life as well), everyone has an opinion. One may find you too quiet; another may find you to be too talkative. Read the social cues in the situation and follow up accordingly with that person.

When you speak, wait for a response. See how he is reacting to what you are saying. You can often tell when a person is losing interest if that person is no longer maintaining eye contact with you or begins to shuffle through papers instead of paying attention.

Of course, being "too aggressive" is never a good thing. We all want to be 'heard' in the interview but you have to present your message professionally and calmly in the right context to make the best impression. Just like in sales, it is not only what you say but how and when you say it.

KNOWING WHERE YOU ARE GOING

After you have spent days on research and practicing for your interview, you want to avoid any hiccups that could occur the day of your interview. The first steps to avoiding that is knowing where you are going and how long it will take to get there.

If you are unfamiliar with the geographic location, give yourself plenty of extra time to get there or even consider doing a dry run to the location- practice going to the interview location a day or two beforehand. By learning your way around in advance, you can alleviate any travel related stress such as taking the wrong turn or getting on the wrong train.

Allow yourself twice the amount of time that you expect that you will need to arrive at your location on time. For example, if google maps shows you a travel time of half an hour, leave yourself an hour to travel to your interview. You don't want to stress every time there is a missed bus connection or traffic up ahead.

When you arrive near your location with plenty of time to spare, try to find a place to relax, clear your mind or even review some notes. You may want to look for a quiet coffee house nearby.

Arrive at your interview location no sooner than 15 minutes before your scheduled interview time. You don't want to seem desperate or appear as if you have nothing else do. Arriving 10 to 15 minutes early will allow you to pass through security and complete an application before your scheduled interview time.

YOUR RESUME ON THE INTERVIEW

After a company has received our resume and perhaps given us a phone interview, we often make a reasonable assumption. The assumption is that the same company that grilled us over the phone about our skills, background and qualifications after having received our resume via email, will keep that same resume handy on the day we are invited in for the interview.

This is a faulty assumption. The company expects you to act professionally during the interview process and one of those expectations is that you bring a copy of your resume. Not only should you bring one copy of your resume, bring several. You may be asked to hand in a copy for their files with your application and give the interviewer another copy. It may be a multi-person interview or you may be asked to stay to meet with additional decision makers. It never hurts to be prepared, so have those extra copies ready.

Printing a resume on fancy paper has become a bit passé these days. As long as you have a few clean copies available on white copier paper, you will be fine. Have a folder or over the shoulder bag where you can store the copies.

Our resume is the advertisement of our skills, experience and abilities for the job. Once someone has called you in for an interview, the resume has done the job it needed to do: Get your foot in the door and allow you to sell yourself in-person.

There is no reason to bring a resume different than the one you had used to apply for the job in the first place. I don't care how good the new resume is. By adding new information or repositioning the content, it may make you appear overqualified for the job when you hadn't before or the information that captured the interviewer's interest will no longer be emphasized.

When you are asked on the interview if you brought a copy of the resume, just provide the one that you submitted originally to avoid any unforeseen hurdles.

2 MASTER YOUR PHONE INTERVIEW

Being interviewed over the phone is a unique and challenging experience. In a limited amount of time, you have to be prepared to sell your appropriateness for the opportunity in order to secure a spot in the next round of interviews. In order to succeed, you will need to understand the different types of phone interviews you may encounter, how to respond most appropriately to the questions asked and what to do in order to gain clarity for the next steps in the process.

So, what is a phone interview? Of course, it is an interview that takes place over the phone but there are a few permutations of the phone interview to prepare for. Sometimes, you may not even realize that you are being interviewed.

The role of the person on the phone is often that of recruiter. The first type of phone interview is not really an interview at all: a recruiter contacting you with the intention of setting up an-in person interview. The recruiter would like to confirm your interest in the position and provide you with the details of when your interview will take place and who you will be meeting with. The recruiter has every intention of setting up an interview for you at this point unless you give her a reason to be concerned.

There could be variety of reasons that the phone call is eliciting concern on the recruiter's behalf such as:

- You answered the call in an unprofessional manner and seem confused as to why you are receiving a phone call. You may not be expecting a call and you are treating the recruiter like a telemarketer until you figure out what the call is concerning.

- You seem uninterested in interviewing for the position.

- You are asking several basic questions about the job, demonstrating that you do not remember much of anything about the company or the role.

- You do not sound professional on the phone. Perhaps you are too focused on the salary or the hours for the position or you are being too candid or lax in your language.

- You cannot be heard or understood. You may be in an area with bad cell phone reception or trying to whisper at your current place or employment or your kids are trying to talk over you when you are on the phone.

As a recent college graduate several years ago, I attempted to answer a call in Times Square from a recruiter representing a large media company. Needless to say, one of the busiest places in the world was (and is) one of the loudest as well. After a few responses of "Can you repeat that?" the opportunity was lost. I was told by the recruiter that he would call me back but that never happened.

- You are inflexible in your availability to come in for an interview. The recruiter may have proposed several times for you to attend an in-person interview but none of those times work for you due to your work schedule or other commitments.

While the recruiter may have called you with every intention of setting up an interview, a point or two of concern may have eliminated your chances. You will be told that you will be contacted once the company has made a decision rather than being called in for an interview.

In some cases, the recruiter attempted to reach you but was unsuccessful in doing so or experienced an area of concern that eliminated that possibility. That may include:

- An unprofessional voicemail message. Your first verbal impression might be your voicemail message so make sure that it is professionally appropriate. Provide a message that clearly states your name that you are sorry that you missed the call and that you will return the call as soon as time allows. Avoid any voicemails messages that include extended words of inspiration, attempts at demonstrating your vocal or rap talents or allowing your kids to record a cute message on your behalf.

- A voicemail message that is not in English or you do not state your name. The recruiter has to know that she reached you. Always provide your name in your message and if you expect that many of the callers to your phone are non-English speakers, provide at least a message in your language of preference as well as one in English.

- Your phone is out of order. Whether it is a permanent change in number or you have used up your prepaid minutes, an out of service phone will lead to a missed opportunity. Unless you possess unique skills that are unlikely to be found in other candidates (and even then), a recruiter is not going to chase you down to find you on social media or email.

- Someone answering the phone who does not take a message for you with all of the necessary details.

So, how can you ensure a smooth phone screening and no stumbling blocks to the in-person interview?

- If you do not recognize the phone number, assume that it may be a recruiter. Answer the call with your name and in a professional manner.

- Be prepared to talk when you answer the phone. If you are unprepared to talk, let the phone go to voicemail.

- If you are prepared to talk but you see that your cell phone reception is very weak or your train is about to go underground, let the call go to voicemail.

- If you planned to be able to talk but something came up unexpectedly, take the recruiter's name and number, and ask when you may call back.

- When you are job seeking, you should have a general idea of your schedule of availability so that setting up an in-person interview is not an arduous process.

- It would be difficult to access every application you have made over the last few months in order to be prepared every time the phone rings but it would be helpful to maintain a basic list that you can quickly peruse for information to refresh your memory once you are contacted.

- If you absolutely have to, fake it until you make it. Make it clear that you are interested in the opportunity when speaking on the phone until you have a reason not to be interested. Do your best to show enthusiasm while you are trying to figure things out.

By following the suggestions above, you will be able to avoid the pitfalls of the seemingly "simple" process of setting up the interview when the recruiter calls you.

All conditions being perfect, it is best to answer the call then and there but sometimes it is not the ideal time. It may be difficult to reach the recruiter later but it is better than to pick up the phone in a bad reception zone or a noisy area.

The next style of phone interview is a pre-screening, which involves being asked a handful of questions to determine if you match the basic criteria needed for the role. The recruiter is trying to avoid having to meet in-person with candidates who are clearly not a fit for the job.

One of the challenges of this type of phone interview is that you may or may not be given a warning in advance. Some recruiters may email you to set up a time for a brief phone screening whereas others will just launch into their questions. What this means is that you must always be prepared. These brief few minutes are your opportunity to sell yourself for the role. The recruiter will not give much consideration to whatever was going on at the time of the call that may have been a distraction to you or hurt your chances of putting your best foot forward.

While you cannot anticipate all of the questions that may be asked, the questions do tend to veer to the basics during a phone screen. A recruiter will generally not have an expert knowledge of the position that you are interviewing for. He will be looking for a basic skills match and looking to weed out people with major question marks in their backgrounds.

The key here is that time is limited. The recruiter is trying to determine your basic fit for the role. Similar questions may be asked by the same person during an in person interview, which you can answer with greater depth and detail at that time.

No matter what questions are asked, consider the following:

How can I demonstrate that I am a great fit for this role when I answer this question? An interview isn't about you but an opportunity to show why you are a great fit for the job.

Without having the opportunity to see someone in person, there is a connection that is lost over the phone. Try to project a good level of energy and enthusiasm over the phone. If normally you are subdued and a quiet talker, you may need to push yourself outside of your comfort zone for the phone interview. In order to project your voice and maintain your enthusiasm, you may want to stand up for the phone interview and speak a bit louder than you normally would. Although it might be tempting, avoid pacing around. Your phone might hit certain bad reception areas if you are walking around so avoid having the phone cut in and out.

If you are given the opportunity to prepare for the phone screening, there are several steps that you can take to put your best foot forward:

Research: When you know that you have a phone screening to prepare for, don't be reliant upon remembering what you learned about the company when you submitted your resume. Look up the company website and read current articles about the organization.

Review: Reread the job description for the position (you saved it, right? If not, a Google search might help you to find the old posting), the cover letter that you sent as well as your resume.

Consider: What questions you might be asked about your background and determine how you can explain any bumps in your career journey- such as an inconsistent work history or if you have ever been fired.

If you need to, admit to any mistakes or errors in judgment but focus on what you have learned as well. Try to stay light on the negativity and focus on the positive.

Space: Find a quiet area where you will be taking the call. If you are at home, make sure that your family knows that you have an important call at that time and you will let them know when you are off of the phone.

Do not ask about the salary over the phone. Just like it is not appropriate to ask about the salary during your first in person interview, it is not appropriate to ask here either.

The recruiter might ask what salary you are seeking as a way to weed out candidates over the phone. Provide a wide salary range as opposed to a number. Once you have responded, you can inquire as to what range the company has in mind.

When you are asked if you have any questions, don't focus on the hours of the job or the fringe benefits. Use this as your opportunity to gain clarity on the next steps in the process as well as the recruiter's contact information.

Ask what are the next steps in the process and when you can expect to hear back. This will provide you with a timeline for your follow up strategy. If you are told that you will hear back within two weeks, it would be acceptable for you to contact the recruiter again somewhere in the range of two and a half to three weeks later.

Make sure to get the recruiter's full name and email address. Email the recruiter a thank you note within one day of your phone interview. Avoid a generic note that can be used for anyone at any time. Include a couple of specific details that were discussed and a reference as to your strong qualifications.

"Dear Ms. Thomas,

Thank you for taking the time over the phone to discuss the position of Systems Analyst. I enjoyed learning more about the organization's planned expansion into the South American market. Given my knowledge of the region and relevant experience in the areas of banking and finance, I am excited to learn more. I am looking forward to the next steps in the process.

Regards"

The third, and final, type of phone interview is not a pre-screening but your actual "first interview". The most common reason that the first interview takes place over the phone is for logistical purposes: candidates from outside of the geographic area are being considered for the position and to be respectful of everyone's time, the phone interview is replacing the need to travel to an in-person interview. This style of interview is becoming less commonplace as interviews with remote candidates are more commonly being conducted over Skype or similar web based application.

Being able to participate in a formal interview over the phone does have some advantages for the applicant. As you cannot be seen by the interviewer, you can keep your notes in front of you. This might include a list of the questions that you want to ask, reminders of particular accomplishments that you want to be sure to mention and possibly even your resume.

If there is more than one person on the other end of the line, you have to pay special attention as to when it is your time to talk. The first interviewer may have just finished talking and you are ready to respond but the second interviewer has something to say. When there is more than one interviewer, allow a brief moment before you respond to each question before you respond.

As opposed to a briefer pre-screening interview, you should provide answers that go more in-depth and paint a picture of your strong qualifications for the job.

3 WINNING INTERVIEW ANSWERS: YOUR BACKGROUND

Tell me about yourself.

<u>Why this question is being asked</u>: The interviewer would like to know about the professional you and understand your qualifications for the job.

<u>Strategy</u>: Focus on the professional you. The interviewer does not want to know about where you took your last vacation or what your favorite pastime is. Provide an introduction to your relevant experience, education, skills and knowledge that will be discussed more in-depth over the course of the interview.

<u>Sample answer</u>: I am a Public Accountant with ten years of experience in the field. I recently received my CPA. For the last 6 years, I've worked for Smithson Auditors in a senior capacity. Prior to that, I worked for Jacoby Accounting. Supervisors have described me as a quick learner and a great team player.

What major challenges and problems did you face in your last job?

<u>Why this question is being asked</u>: Jobs are full of challenges. The interviewer would like to know how you have handled problems or challenges in the past as you are likely to face obstacles in this job as well.

Strategy: Demonstrate how you can overcome a challenge. Provide an example of a problem or challenge that would have relevance for the interviewer and show how you overcame that challenge. In structuring your answer, provide the problem followed by the action and then the result.

Sample answer: Two years ago, my employer acquired a niche firm. This created natural friction between long-time employees and those who came aboard during the acquisition. Each team had their own way of doing things. At the beginning, having more employees slowed down our ability to finish projects successfully due to miscommunication and conflict. After this happened, I asked members of our team to meet me for lunch. We went out in a relaxed atmosphere and began to discuss our working styles and why we work the way we do. It opened the line of communications and we began to understand each other better. This led to better teamwork in the future.

How would someone who dislikes you describe you?

Why this question is being asked: The interviewer wants to understand how you deal with a question that is unexpected and makes you acknowledge that you are not perfect.

Strategy: Acknowledge the answer. Do not try and avoid it by saying, "Everyone likes me". Be cautious not to provide anything negative about yourself but think of different work styles and why someone with a conflicting work style may not like you.

Sample answer: Wow. That is a good question as I normally would not focus on negative thoughts or think about people not liking me in a professional context but if I had to give an answer, I would say, "I don't like working with him as I like to take things as they come and charge into a problem and he likes to think things through too much. He likes to create a plan and analyze the situation thoroughly before diving in and that is frustrating to me."

What was your biggest failure?

<u>Why this question is being asked</u>: Not everything will go your way all of the time and the interviewer wants to understand how you will handle it when things don't go right.

<u>Strategy</u>: Acknowledge the question. Do not try and avoid it by saying, "I have never failed". Provide a relevant failure and explain what you have learned from it that makes you a better professional today.

<u>Sample answer</u>: Early in my career, I overextended myself to grow my professional capabilities. I was working full-time and also attending a master's program at night and on the weekends. It was manageable until I received a promotion at work. I felt overwhelmed and left the master's program at the end of the semester. It felt like a failure because I could have given it more time to work out the responsibilities. I've learned to consider things more carefully before making any final decisions. As an aside, I've just restarted my master's and things are going really well!

What is your definition of failure?

<u>Why this question is being asked</u>: Working in a job is all about meeting objectives. The interviewer wants to understand how you judge things like success and failure.

<u>Strategy</u>: Provide some insight into your working style in a way that would be appealing for the interviewer.

<u>Sample answer</u>: To me, failure is not even trying. Sometimes there are opportunities given by a supervisor that one can take if he or she is willing to take on the challenge. Many people are so afraid of failure that they are afraid to even try challenging assignments. Failure is not trying something and it not working out. For me, not trying something out of my comfort zone would be the failure.

What are your regrets?

<u>Why this question is being asked</u>: Not everything will go your way all of the time and the interviewer needs to understand how you will handle it when things don't go right.

<u>Strategy</u>: Acknowledge the question. Provide a regret you may have that is relevant to the job and what you may have learned from it.

<u>Sample answer</u>: I am not the type of person who normally focuses on things like regret as we all make mistakes. It is important to acknowledge those mistakes but then move on. If I did have to focus on one answer, I would say that I regret not being more open to opportunities early in my career. When I was in college, I was laser-focused as to what type of job I wanted. I had the industry, role and even the location all planned out. When I received a call for an interview and it was in an outer borough, I declined the interview because it wasn't what I wanted exactly. I've learned not to be so closed minded to opportunity. In fact, I've become used to commuting for over an hour!

What is your greatest weakness?

<u>Why this question is being asked</u>: In order to gain a better understanding of the "professional you". The interviewer

doesn't want to hear just about what you do well but what you may do poorly as well.

Strategy: Provide a relevant weakness that you may have had, what you have done to overcome it and where you stand now.

Sample answer: I've always considered myself a quieter person. While I am very comfortable talking to people one on one, or even giving presentations, I have always been intimidated to go over to people I do not know and introduce myself. Given my role in the business world, I knew that I had to get beyond that. I've made a concerted effort to put myself out there and meet new people. While it can be intimidating to do so, I don't think anyone notices that I am uncomfortable sometimes and I've made some great new connections.

When was the last time you were angry?

Why this question is being asked: The interviewer wants to learn how you manage your emotions on the job and if you can maintain your professionalism.

Strategy: Acknowledge the question. Do not try to say that you never get angry but provide a relevant example and share what you learned from it.

Sample answer: As a professional, I try to stay away from being angry at a co-worker or a client. Sometimes, someone may do something upsetting but I try to manage my emotions. One example does come to mind though. Early in my career, I shared a cubicle with someone in a similar capacity to me. As a worker, I tend to be all-in about my work and being a professional. This person was just about the opposite. He would be on inappropriate websites, make personal phone calls and even fall asleep when we were asked to meet with clients. The last part was especially upsetting as it was not only him acting unprofessionally; it was becoming a reflection on me. Eventually, he was caught for his behavior while I was able to take on additional responsibilities and move away from my association with him.

If you could relive the last 10 years of your life, what would you do differently?

<u>Why this question is being asked</u>: The interviewer wants to get a sense of where you are going with your career by having you reflect on your past.

<u>Strategy</u>: Focus on what you've learned through your experience and if you had known, what you would have done differently.

<u>Sample answer</u>: I am not the type of person that lives with a great deal of regret. I try to be thoughtful about my actions, but we all make mistakes. One of the things I would have done differently, but I could have only learned through the experiences that I did have, was to be more culturally sensitive. I've worked with many people from a variety of backgrounds and if I would have understood their perspectives based on their experiences better, I think we could have worked more effectively together.

Tell me about a time when you helped resolve a dispute between others.

Why this question is being asked: Conflicting opinions and strong personalities are often a part of the workplace. People that can take on leadership roles and resolve problems are heavily valued.

Strategy: Provide an example where you can demonstrate your leadership abilities to resolve a conflict. Explain what was the problem, the action that you took and the end result.

Sample answer: As an accounts manager, I had taken on a mentoring role for two relatively new employees. They were working closely together, and a conflict arose as to which one should get the credit for securing the account. They agreed to talk it out with me before going to the supervisor. Upon hearing each other's side of the situation, they agreed that each deserved some credit and realized that to find mutual success in their new roles, they would be best served by working together.

What are your goals?

Why this question is being asked: The interviewer wants to know if your goals align with those of the organization.

Strategy: Focus on an "everybody wins" approach as opposed to only what you want. Be specific as to the items relevant to the industry that you would like to accomplish but avoid naming a specific job title.

Sample answer: I want to continue to contribute to a media organization in a meaningful way. My exact job title is not as important to me as the type of work that I would be doing. I know that if I can contribute positively, the company will benefit and we will all win in the end.

What is your dream job?

Why this question is being asked: The interviewer wants to know if your dreams and goals align with those of the organization.

Strategy: Focus on job duties relevant to the industry in which you are applying. Avoid naming a specific job title. Paint a realistic picture.

Sample answer: I look for the potential in most things, so any job that I've held has had pieces of a dream job to me. I understand that even the ideal job will have stress at certain times and various challenges, big and small, to overcome. For me the ideal job is when I can continue to contribute to a media organization in a meaningful, progressively responsible way.

What are two things your former manager would like you to improve on?

Why this question is being asked: The interviewer is looking for you to be candid and share professional aspects about yourself that may not be your strong suits.

Strategy: Focus on aspects of yourself that may have been places for improvement earlier in your career. Show how you have overcome those weaknesses and where you are today.

Sample answer: The supervisor in my first job had a difficult personality so I have a good sense of how to answer this one.

"He has poor communication skills." He felt that I could not communicate well and should not speak on the phone. Although I felt this was partly because I am naturally quieter when acclimating to a situation, I did take steps to improve my communication abilities. I've been attending toastmaster meetings for the last 5 years. This has improved my public speaking abilities greatly and speaking publicly is a major part of what I do.

"He is not a leader." I can understand why my first boss had this initial perception of me. As I mentioned, in my first role, I was quieter and intimidated to speak out too much. I just focused on the work. As I've grown as a professional, so have my leadership abilities. Even in that job, I helped to train new employees and was left in charge of overseeing the office in the absence of a supervisor. As I've grown in my career, I have often taken on the role of team leader.

Tell me about an accomplishment you are most proud of.

<u>Why this question is being asked</u>: By learning about what you've accomplished in the past, the interviewer has a better sense of what you may accomplish in the future.

<u>Strategy</u>: Paint a picture with your words of an accomplishment that would be relevant to the position for which you are applying.

<u>Sample answer</u>: I was called upon to do a job meant for two people. I was able not only to meet the demands of both positions, but to really excel. As the company acquired various new businesses, the CEO was looking for someone who already had experience in account management to lead a new team. I was asked to do so while maintaining my old position as well. I would spend two and a half days at each site per week. Through maximizing resources, especially leaning on technology as a communication tool, I was able to stay on top of both roles and exceed expectations.

Are you a leader or a follower?

<u>Why this question is being asked</u>: The interviewer wants to understand how you'd fit into the organization given your role.

<u>Strategy</u>: Every organization values some leadership qualities but wants someone who will follow directives as well. Try to maintain a balance between the two.

<u>Sample answer</u>: I take a leadership role on those occasions that call for expertise or experience that I have and which my colleagues may not possess. I am always ready to share my knowledge. But as a leader, I understand that sometimes it important to be a good follower as well in order to learn from others.

What are some of your leadership experiences?

<u>Why this question is being asked</u>: As the ability to lead is an important quality no matter what your role, the interviewer wants to know more about your ability to lead by learning if you have done so in the past.

<u>Strategy</u>: Provide a memorable story (or two) that demonstrates your leadership qualities. It is better to provide only one or two stories than to provide a laundry list of all of your leadership experiences, with none being memorable following the interview.

<u>Sample answer</u>: Every quarter, my department has to provide a report on its accomplishments to the executives. I volunteered for the role of team lead in gathering this information from co-workers and ensuring that it was as accurate and organized as possible. I called several team meetings to set objectives and deadlines for our work and

met with individual members to answer any questions and to make sure we were on the same page. We produced a report that was praised by the executive team and I have been the go-to person ever since.

Why aren't you earning more money at this stage of your career?

<u>Why this question is being asked</u>: The interviewer wants to understand how much the salary factors in to your career goals.

<u>Strategy</u>: Explain your long term strategy in preparing yourself for the highest future earnings as opposed to taking whatever highest paying job comes next.

<u>Sample answer</u>: Up to this point in my career, it has been all about contributing to the organization and getting as much experience as possible. I chose to take some jobs that paid in the middle range of the market as opposed to the highest, as I knew those firms would challenge me the most and I'd have the best opportunity to learn. Now that I've gained all of that experience, I feel that I am in the position to pursue a job that adequately meets both of my goals- to challenge me as well as pay a salary that is at the higher end of the scale.

Who has inspired you in your life and why?

Why this question is being asked: As the interviewer does not know you, he/she wants to understand what made you the person that you are.

Strategy: Provide a few examples of family, friends and/or mentors who've inspired you through their work ethic and dedication to a task.

Sample answer: It would be difficult not to be inspired by one's parents. Thankfully, mine served as great role models for me. In addition to dedicating their free time to their children, they have a tremendous work ethic. My father would wake up extra early to get to work earlier in order to put in extra hours so that he could get home in time to see his kids. If need be, he returned to work after we had gone to bed.

What techniques and tools do you use to keep yourself organized?

Why this question is being asked: In a world of increasing demands, multi-tasking and reporting, the interviewer would like to know how you remain organized.

Strategy: Everyone has different strategies but paint a picture of a person that is organized and has created a system to stay on top of the work.

Sample answer: The first thing that I do is create a running task list for myself in Google docs. In that list, I place deadlines and notes as to my progress. I have a calendar app for all of my appointments and to-do's as well as a physical appointment calendar as a backup. I like to arrive early to the office to clear out my inbox and voicemail system and solidify a working plan for the day.

What is your personal mission statement?

<u>Why this question is being asked</u>: The interviewer wants to understand what defines you in order to determine how you would fit into the company culture.

<u>Strategy</u>: Provide a well-defined mission statement that demonstrates your strong work ethic, moral compass and drive to succeed. Consider the mission statement of the company and make sure that it is compatible with your own.

<u>Sample answer</u>: To utilize my strong work ethic and drive to succeed to meet my own objectives, as well as those of people who count on me, in a responsible and morally appropriate way.

What is your greatest achievement outside of work?

<u>Why this question is being asked</u>: The employer wants to understand who you are as a person outside of a job setting.

<u>Strategy</u>: Focus on an achievement that demonstrate experiences, skills or abilities that was performed outside of the job.

<u>Sample answer</u>: I've been volunteering for an organization called Building Homes for the Homeless since 1999. At first, I was just a helper when we went into a town and helped to actually build a home. I've worked my way up and I'm now the team leader. It's a great feeling to successfully lead others in volunteering their time for such a worthy cause.

Tell me one thing about yourself you wouldn't want me to know.

<u>Why this question is being asked</u>: The interviewer wants to

know how you'll handle a question that you did not anticipate and what you'll say that you may not have planned to.

<u>Strategy</u>: Don't provide an actual weakness about yourself. Provide something that you may not have really said otherwise but makes you seem like a stronger candidate.

<u>Sample answer</u>: Well to be honest, I've actually been following this company for a long time. I'm a fan of your work. I know that you aren't looking to hire someone that is just a fan but is also a great fit and employee and I think that I'm an excellent balance between the two.

What is your favorite memory from your teenage years?

<u>Why this question is being asked</u>: The employer wants to understand more of who you are as a person.

<u>Strategy</u>: Provide something that shows your good character and would be applicable to making you a better professional.

<u>Sample answer</u>: My favorite memory was watching my sister graduate from high school. She struggled with her math classes and she wasn't sure she was going to be able to pass. I tutored her and she became more confident. A few months later, my sister made a copy of her diploma and gave it to me with a note of thanks.

What accomplishment has given you the most satisfaction?

<u>Why this question is being asked</u>: A predictor of your ability to accomplish things in the future is partly based on what you've accomplished in the past.

<u>Strategy</u>: Provide an accomplishment that would be relevant to the job you are interviewing for. Paint a picture of what you accomplished, how you went about accomplishing it and why it was important.

<u>Sample answer</u>: I've always been good at multi-tasking but I was not sure that I'd be able to go to school full-time while working and raising a family. It wasn't always easy but I was able to do it successfully. I'd study on the train, wake up early, go to sleep late and learned how to manage everything that I do more effectively.

What are your hobbies?

<u>Why this question is being asked</u>: The interviewer wants to understand who you are outside of the job.

<u>Strategy</u>: There is really no wrong answer here but you should avoid any controversial answers. This is not really the place to discuss hunting or governmental protests.

<u>Sample answer</u>: Since my job is desk-based, I like to do hobbies that give me exercise and allow me to spend time with my family. I like to play sports and go camping.

What sports do you play?

<u>Why this question is being asked</u>: The interviewer wants to understand who you are outside of the job. There is some perception that active, healthier people are more productive.

<u>Strategy</u>: If possible, provide some examples of sports you participate in to show that you are active and are not all about work. To show a competitive spirit isn't a bad thing either.

<u>Sample answer</u>: Informally, I run regularly. I like to compete with myself in breaking my fastest time. I have a competitive spirit so when time allows, I like to participate in pickup basketball games.

What kind of games do you like to play?

<u>Why this question is being asked</u>: The interviewer wants to better understand who you are outside of the job.

<u>Strategy</u>: Focus on games that require solving puzzles and strategic thinking as these are valued skills in most jobs.

<u>Sample answer</u>: I enjoy playing chess. It's the type of game that no matter how skilled you become, there is always someone better. It motivates me to continue to learn and improve.

What do you do in your leisure time?

<u>Why this question is being asked</u>: The interviewer wants to know if you are a well rounded person.

<u>Strategy</u>: There is really no wrong answer here but you should avoid any controversial answers. This is not really the place to discuss hunting or governmental protests.

<u>Sample answer</u>: I dedicate much of my time to my job but I find that it is important to find the time to relax. I enjoy spending time with my wife and daughter. We like to go to the park, see friends and go out to eat.

What do you do to deal with stress?

<u>Why this question is being asked</u>: As work is naturally stressful, the interviewer wants to know how you manage yours.

<u>Strategy</u>: Be honest that you do get stressed. Provide concrete examples to show how you can manage the stress.

<u>Sample answer</u>: I try to remain calm and prioritize my time when thinking about what needs to be done first. If it is an especially stressful time of year, I make sure to spend my lunch away from my desk and to get some exercise. I find that it makes me feel refreshed so that I have the energy to deal with the work.

What do you do to help balance life and work?

<u>Why this question is being asked</u>: The interviewer wants to know if you are a well rounded person.

<u>Strategy</u>: Provide concrete examples of how you maintain that balance. The interviewer is likely to be unimpressed if you say that you cannot maintain that balance and that you are a workaholic.

<u>Sample answer</u>: It can be difficult to maintain a proper balance but I think I manage it. For me the key is maximizing my time. On the train on the way to work, I am preparing for work and on the way home, I'm preparing for the next day as well. That way, I can mitigate the need to stay late at the

office and spend time with my family. Plus, the weekends are family time (unless there is something essential to take care of before Monday rolls around).

Would you rather be liked or feared?

<u>Why this question is being asked</u>: The interviewer would like to get a better sense of your management style.

<u>Strategy</u>: Find a balance for a middle ground. If you only say that you want to be liked, the interviewer might think you are a pushover and if you say that you need to be feared, you'll come off as a dictator.

<u>Sample answer</u>: I would want to be liked because I am a respected leader who leads by example. As an effective leader, my team would be fearful of not doing their best because each would know that everyone has put in a great effort and no one wants to disappoint the team.

How competitive are you?

<u>Why this question is being asked</u>: Most jobs require a certain amount of competition, either between employees or externally, and the interviewer would like to see how you hold up.

<u>Strategy</u>: Provide clear examples that show you thrive on a good amount of competition but that you wouldn't do anything, especially if it is unethical, to get ahead.

<u>Sample answer</u>: I do enjoy a healthy competition. I find that competing with co-workers motivates us all to be better. If someone comes up with a great strategy or technique that works well, the next person can build on that and we can all grow.

Tell me about a time when you used your creativity to overcome a problem.

<u>Why this question is being asked</u>: There isn't always a guidebook to solve all of the problems that can, and do, arise at work. The interviewer wants to know if you can be creative in order to solve problems.

<u>Strategy</u>: Provide an example relevant to the job you are applying for. Describe the problem, the creative approach you used to solve the problem and what the positive end result was.

<u>Sample answer</u>: I have to establish relationships with executives. The most difficult part is reaching them. I've learned how to find any email address at a company when you can find that of one person. I google for the email address of anyone at the company to learn how their system works. Once I have that along with an executive's name, I can contact him or her directly. This has led to a much higher rate of response than trying to reach the person on the phone or through an intermediary.

Which of your technical skills has most helped you on the job?

<u>Why this question is being asked:</u> Technical aptitude is an increasing important skill no matter what your role. The interviewer would like to get a better understanding of your strongest skills.

<u>Strategy</u>: Provide a technical skill relevant to the job you are pursuing. Demonstrate your expertise by providing an example of how you used it and why you were successful.

<u>Sample answer</u>: I have a good understanding of how to utilize social media. I've trained our sales staff in the use of

LinkedIn to increase company visibility.

What new skills have you learned or developed recently?

<u>Why this question is being asked</u>: The interviewer would like to know if you are a lifelong learner. Companies want to hire people that are constantly learning and not stagnating.

<u>Strategy</u>: Provide an example of something you learned recently that is relevant to the job you are interviewing for. Explain how what you've learned is relevant to your job and what you accomplished.

<u>Sample answer</u>: I recently learned more about the importance of body language. It helped me to better identify what people are communicating with their bodies even when saying something different. This skill has been very helpful when attending business meetings and establishing new relationships.

What sort of things have you done to become better qualified for your career?

<u>Why this question is being asked</u>: The interviewer would like to know if you are a lifelong learner. Companies want to hire people that are constantly learning and not stagnating.

<u>Strategy</u>: Provide a relevant example of how you have continued to learn and improve to become a better qualified learner.

<u>Sample answer</u>: I believe that it is important to keep learning in order to improve and I participate in as many professional development opportunities as possible. I attend two or three conferences a year in my field. I participate in cross-trainings from other departments at my current job. Additionally, I am

an active contributor in several relevant LinkedIn groups.

What were your responsibilities in your last job?

<u>Why this question is being asked</u>: The interviewer would like to know if the job you are currently pursuing is similar to your last job or if it would be a step up in increased responsibilities.

<u>Strategy</u>: Consider the responsibilities of the job you are pursuing when describing your previous job. The objective is to demonstrate that you can handle the responsibilities of the new job because you've done most of them already in your old job.

<u>Sample answer</u>: From my understanding of this job, many of the responsibilities of my previous job would have been similar including….

What have you done to improve your knowledge in the last year?

<u>Why this question is being asked</u>: The interviewer would like to know if you are a lifelong learner. Companies want to hire people that are constantly learning and not stagnating.

<u>Strategy</u>: Provide a few examples relevant examples of how you have continued to learn and improve to become a better qualified learner.

<u>Sample answer</u>: I believe that it is important to keep learning in order to improve and I participate in as many professional development opportunities as possible. I attend two or three conferences a year in my field. I participate in cross-trainings from other departments at my current job. Additionally, I am an active contributor in several relevant LinkedIn groups.

Do you have a favorite quote? What is it?

<u>Why this question is being asked</u>: By requesting your favorite quote, the interviewer will be able to gain better insight into the type of person you are.

<u>Strategy</u>: Quotes can be quite powerful. What you interpret a quote to mean can be quite different from what someone else thinks it means. Be careful to select something that is not too revealing personally or shows a leaning towards controversial opinions. If possible, select something about leadership or a strong work ethic. Explain why you selected it and what it means to you.

<u>Sample answer</u>: I heard this one as a teenager when I was still trying to figure out what I wanted to be. It is a quote by Bruce Springsteen, "My parents always told me to get a little something for myself. What they didn't know was, was that I wanted everything". It inspired me to reach higher for my goals and not to settle. I knew that it wouldn't be easy but if I maintained a strong work ethic, I could achieve what I wanted.

Who is your role model and why?

<u>Why this question is being asked</u>: As the interviewer does not know you, he/she wants to understand what made you the person that you are.

<u>Strategy</u>: Provide an example of a family member, friend or mentor who served as a role model to you through his/her work ethic and dedication to a task.

<u>Sample answer</u>: It would be difficult not to be inspired by one's parents. Thankfully, mine served as great role models for me. In addition to dedicating their free time to their children, they have a tremendous work ethic. My father would wake up extra early to get to work earlier in order to put in extra hours so that he could get home in time to see his kids. If need be, he returned to work after we had gone to bed.

Who do you respect? Why?

<u>Why this question is being asked</u>: Part of any job is showing respect for the people that you work with and the employer wants to understand if you are respectful of others.

<u>Strategy</u>: Explain that you are respectful of everybody and can work with anybody as opposed to someone needing to earn your respect.

<u>Sample answer</u>: I think it is important to respect everybody. Although some people might appear more accomplished than others, and more worthy of respect, we don't know everyone's story and how they got to be who they are. When we start on an even playing ground of respecting everybody, without feeling that someone has to earn our respect first, we

are more likely to create stronger bonds and better working relationships.

Tell me about someone you admire and why?

<u>Why this question is being asked</u>: As the interviewer does not know you, he/she wants to understand what made you the person that you are.

<u>Strategy</u>: Provide an example of a mentor who has inspired you through his/her work ethic and dedication to a task.

<u>Sample answer</u>: My first supervisor, Jane Riley, was an inspiration for me. She has a tremendous moral compass. If something appeared morally questionable, she taught us to lean towards the right thing to do. She was right as it strengthened our relationship with clients and benefited everyone in the end.

What unique experiences separate you from other candidates?

<u>Why this question is being asked</u>: The interviewer wants to know why you should be hired instead of someone else.

<u>Strategy</u>: Focus on building yourself up, instead of knocking others down. This is your chance give the strongest pitch possible for yourself.

<u>Sample answer</u>: I can't speak for the other candidates but I know why I'd be a great fit for this job. I am the right choice because I have a 15 year track record of taking on progressively responsible roles in the field, exceeding objectives and growing the business. I have always been counted on to represent my company, train others and assist wherever needed. I continue to learn and improve my skills by taking advantage of any relevant continuing education

opportunities. Although I have a history of success, I am still hungry to meet new goals and overcome challenges. I've followed your company closely for many years and I know that we can be partners together in success.

What kind of person would you refuse to work with?

<u>Why this question is being asked</u>: The interviewer wants to know who you will be able to work with successfully and who you will not.

<u>Strategy</u>: Show openness to working with everybody. If there are difficult personalities, explain why that may be challenging but how you'd make it work.

<u>Sample answer</u>: As I am not the CEO, it is not my choice to say that I will or will not work with someone. I will always do my best to make it work. Now, are there difficult personalities to deal with in any job? Sure. Who would I prefer not to work with? If I had to say, the two types of people that come to mind are those who are know-it-alls and those who are liars. It is difficult to have open communication with either type of person. But I would trust that the company put them in their roles because they contribute to the organization and I'd figure out a way to make it work. The most important thing is open communication and when I encounter a problem, I'd ask for open dialogue to clear the air.

What are your short-range goals and objectives, when and why did you establish these goals and how are you preparing yourself to achieve them?

<u>Why this question is being asked</u>: The interviewer would like to determine if your goals match the company goals.

<u>Strategy</u>: Consider the job you are applying for and provide an answer that would be appropriate for someone in that role.

<u>Sample answer</u>: I'd like to move from my role as a Media Buyer into a Senior Media Buyer. This will allow me to meet some of my short range goals of contributing more dynamically to a company, learning more about the buying side of the business and also having an opportunity to train and mentor junior employees.

Give me an example of an important goal that you set in the past and tell me about your success in reaching it.

<u>Why this question is being asked</u>: Being able to reach your goals is an important part of any job. How you've done in the past is being used as a predictor for how you may do in the future.

<u>Strategy</u>: Describe a goal that you were successful in achieving. Provide a description of how you went about achieving that goal, including challenges you overcame and the end result.

<u>Sample answer</u>: A goal of mine was to secure business meetings with 500 marketing managers over the course of one year in order to introduce them to our new web tool. The challenge was that no one at my company had been able to have meetings with more than 200 people in a year and there

was a limited travel budget. I created a plan that helped to maximize my time and overall reach. Utilizing new technologies like GoToMeeting.com, I was able to interact with my target audience one on one without leaving the office as much, saving valuable time. When I did leave the office, I would use a relevant conference as a geographic hub and meet with as many people as possible there. I would then travel around the conference location and meet with people who were local, so I didn't have to make a separate trip. Also, to build up my contacts, I asked each person that I met with to introduce me to someone else. Not only did I reach my goal but I exceeded it as I ended up meeting with 540 marketing managers last year.

What do you really want to do in life?

<u>Why this question is being asked</u>: The interviewer is trying to determine if this job fits into your overall plan. It is helpful for understanding how happy, and ultimately how successful, you will be.

<u>Strategy</u>: Place your answer within the context of the job you are applying for. Create an overall impression of what you want to do in life and how this job will help you get there.

<u>Sample answer</u>: I've always loved the field of advertising. The exact role isn't as important to me as the opportunity to get involved in various aspects of the business including the creative side. This role will be a great opportunity to contribute what I know, learn more, improve my track record and hopefully take on additional responsibility.

What are the most important rewards you expect in your career?

<u>Why this question is being asked</u>: The interviewer would like

to know what motivates you and will make you happy in a job.

Strategy: Don't focus only on the financial rewards. Provide examples of what will make you happy on a job that would fit best with the interests of the company.

Sample answer: Of course financial reward is important, but there are other rewards I value as well. I know that when I contribute to a company's success, financial reward follows. But I also see opportunity to gain additional responsibilities as a reward because it means that my employer values my potential to contribute further. I also appreciate being part of a team that is recognized for its achievements.

What are your best skills?

Why this question is being asked: Weighing the skills that you bring to the table is an important part of the decision making process for the interviewer.

Strategy: Focus on the skills that would be most appropriate for the job for which you are interviewing. You don't want to simply name your skills as if you are writing a grocery list. Instead, take this opportunity to explain your proficiency in utilizing each skill on the job.

Sample answer: I am a great communicator. I can present my ideas well in-person, in writing and through social media. I've worked hard to sharpen those skills because I feel that the value of a great idea is lost if I can't present it in a way that others can understand.

I am a real team player. There is no room for a "me first" attitude in the workplace and we all have to work together in order to meet objectives. Once I've completed my work, I'll walk around my department and ask my co-workers if there is anything I can do to help contribute.

What is the most difficult adjustment you have ever had to make?

<u>Why this question is being asked</u>: Change is constant in the workplace and the interviewer wants to know how you have handled it.

<u>Strategy</u>: Provide an example of change relevant to the job you are applying for. Explain what the challenge was, what you did to overcome it and what the end result was.

<u>Sample answer</u>: Change can be difficult but I am always ready to embrace it. In my industry, an important skill to have is the ability to engage clients one-on-one and build rapport in order to strengthen relationships. My company asked all the people in our division to cease all in-person meetings and do what we needed to do on the phone and on the computer. It was challenging at first to find a rapport without meeting face to face. As I shifted into relying on new methods of communication, I soon created fresh strategies for starting conversations with potential clients remotely. In the end, I've been able to interact with more clients using the new strategy and I find that I'm now able to engage clients as well remotely as I have in-person.

What two things are most important to you in a position?

<u>Why this question is being asked</u>: The interviewer would like to know what your expectations of the job are as part of determining if you are an appropriate fit.

<u>Strategy</u>: Consider what are some of the elements of the job you are interviewing for and incorporate that into your

answer.

Sample answer: I can work in many different types of environments, but if I had to choose two important aspects of a position, it would be an environment where I can continue to take on additional responsibilities as I grow in my job and one that is a team based environment, where we can work together to meet objectives.

What are you interested in outside of your career?

Why this question is being asked: The interviewer would like to know the type of person you are outside of your regular job.

Strategy: There isn't a wrong answer here as long as you avoid controversial topics. If you discuss something that would show an additional skill for the job, all the better.

Sample answer: Much of my free time is spent with my family. I do enjoy hiking and spending time outdoors. I also like to collect silent film movie posters

What is the last movie you watched? Did you like it?

Why this question is being asked: The interviewer would like to know the type of person you are outside of your regular job.

Strategy: You may want to demonstrate your analytical mind and interest in a film with a bit of depth as opposed to your fandom of the latest Hollywood shoot 'em up here.

Sample answer: The last movie I saw was "As Good As It Gets". I did enjoy it. It was an intelligently written film starring Jack Nicholson and Helen Hunt from the late 1990's.

Give an example of a time you misjudged someone.

<u>Why this question is being asked</u>: Your ability to interact well with others is an essential aspect to success on a job.

<u>Strategy</u>: Provide clarity into why you misjudged a person, what happened as a result and how the issue was resolved.

<u>Sample answer</u>: I try not to judge a person I don't know, but it can happen on occasion. When a new co-worker joined our division, he seemed to be moving very fast to get noticed by our upper management. He set up meetings with the vice presidents and began giving reports on how we were operating. What I hadn't realized was that he was new to working in our industry and he didn't have a sense of the communication protocol that was established. Once he realized, he was quite embarrassed and became a better team player. He is actually quite humble and not looking to step over anyone.

What have you learned from your mistakes?

<u>Why this question is being asked</u>: You are bound to make mistakes on the job and the interviewer would like to know how you learn from them.

<u>Strategy</u>: Admit to a mistake; explain what you learned and how you are now a better worker for it.

<u>Sample answer</u>: Earlier in my career, when I would get overwhelmed with work, I would try to work as quickly as possible to keep up. This led to a mistake on a spreadsheet as I left out some essential data and it was submitted as is. When it became clear that it was a flawed report, I realized that it is better to take my time and do the job right as opposed to rushing.

Give an example of a time when you made a mistake because you did not listen well to what someone had to say.

<u>Why this question is being asked</u>: You are bound to make mistakes on the job and the interviewer would like to know how you learn from them.

<u>Strategy</u>: Admit to a mistake; explain what you learned and how you are now a better worker for it.

<u>Sample answer</u>: I was asked to run a comparison of sales month to month and create corresponding charts and graphs for a presentation. I jumped into it with gusto. I was excited to show it to my boss until he told me that he only wanted me to run the comparison for the last 3 months, not for the whole year. Unfortunately, I had wasted company time by putting in extra information and not working on something else. I learned to pay more attention next time and to confirm what my supervisor wants before I begin, if it is not clear what is expected.

Describe times when you were not satisfied or pleased with your performance. What did you do about it?

<u>Why this question is being asked</u>: The interviewer wants to know how seriously you take your work and how you hold yourself accountable.

<u>Strategy</u>: Provide an example relevant to the job you are applying for. Explain the work that you did, why you weren't satisfied, what you learned and how you improved.

<u>Sample answer</u>: I was asked to run a competitor analysis. I examined all of the important metrics. My supervisor was satisfied by the report and I was told that it was helpful for making investment decisions. As I learned additional strategies for running a report like this, I became embarrassed at the quality of my work. I realized that I should have included competitors in related markets and not just direct competition. I learned to lean on senior analysts to provide their feedback before I submit a final report.

Describe a time when you had to make a difficult choice between your personal and professional life.

<u>Why this question is being asked</u>: The interviewer would like to understand how you balance your professional and personal life.

<u>Strategy</u>: The interviewer is not looking for you to say that you always prioritize your professional life. Provide an example of a challenging situation that may relate to the job you are applying for. Explain how you resolved the situation to a mutual benefit.

<u>Sample answer</u>: It can be difficult to maintain a balance between professional and personal life. As my daughter is a

toddler, she is usually asleep by 7:30pm so ideally, I would get home while she is still awake. I know that is not always possible so my spouse and I have come up with different ways to make that work. If I know that I will be out that late, I may wake up an hour earlier to spend time with her. I will also discuss with my supervisor what work must be completed in the office or what I may be able to do remotely (instead of staying late). Sometimes, just talking it out with a supervisor helps. When I started my job, two days a week of overtime was mandatory. After six months, I explained to my supervisor that clients were only coming in late one of those nights and suggested being available earlier one morning a week for client convenience instead. This change helped me to be more effective professionally and also to spend more time at home.

What do you do if you can't solve a problem on your own?

Why this question is being asked: The interviewer wants to know how you solve problems that are beyond your own abilities.

Strategy: Explain the process of acknowledging that the problem was out of your area of expertise, how you went about finding someone to help you and what the end result was.

Sample answer: I have served clients in many different regions of the world, but the needs of the banking industry in Australia were uniquely unfamiliar to me. I quickly did my best to acclimate to their needs but I knew that I could not gain the level of expertise needed in just a few days in order to compete for the account. After consulting with my supervisor, I reached out to our division based in New

Zealand, as I knew they would have a better idea of the industry culture. We partnered to gain the account and it worked out great in the end.

How has your job affected your lifestyle?

<u>Why this question is being asked</u>: The interviewer would like to understand how you balance your professional and personal life.

<u>Strategy</u>: Provide examples that demonstrate your strong work ethic and ability to maintain a balance between your personal and professional lives.

<u>Sample answer</u>: Family life is my number one priority, but it has to be balanced around a job. If I am not doing my job and creating a financially sustainable lifestyle for myself and my family, than it would be hard to concentrate on anything else. I don't think of it as my job affecting my lifestyle but more of a balancing of the two. If my job requires me to stay longer at the office certain days, I'll find the opportunity to spend more time with my family that weekend or wake up earlier in the morning.

What was the most useful criticism you received?

<u>Why this question is being asked</u>: The interviewer wants to understand how well you take constructive criticism and what you learned from it.

<u>Strategy</u>: Provide an example of criticism someone gave you that is relevant to the job you are applying for. Make it clear what you learned from the experience.

<u>Sample answer</u>: When I was in college, I had planned to go into the live events marketing field for my career. In an

interview for a summer internship, the director suggested that I reconsider my interest in the field as I would have to commit many evenings, weekend and travel to the position. In considering what I wanted from a career, I refocused my efforts towards brand marketing, and that has been a much better fit.

Cite an example from your personal life when you were dishonest to someone?

<u>Why this question is being asked</u>: The interviewer would like to get a better sense of your moral character.

<u>Strategy</u>: Admit that you have lied before but provide an explanation that is manageable or why it might have been the right thing to do.

<u>Sample answer</u>: A longtime friend made a mistake at work and was fired. He wanted to know if it would hurt his ability to find a job. I knew that it would but his confidence was shot and he was feeling bad for letting down his family. So I lied and told him that it probably would not hurt his chances.

What you have learned ever since you were born?

<u>Why this question is being asked</u>: The interviewer would like to know how you value knowledge and if you are a lifelong learner.

<u>Strategy</u>: Of course, you aren't going to list everything you've ever learned but you may want to emphasize a few of the most important principles you've learned that would be of value to the employer.

<u>Sample answer</u>: Well, we probably wouldn't have time for me to list everything I've ever learned. If I had to cut it down to

the most important things I've learned it would be that you should treat others as you want to be treated, the more that you give the more that you get and that you always have to be open to learning in order to be successful.

Tell me about an incident in your life that shows how you faced a challenge and how you handled it.

<u>Why this question is being asked</u>: Every job has challenges and the interviewer likes to know how you can handle them.

<u>Strategy</u>: Provide a relevant example of an incident that you encountered on the job, how you handled it and what was the end result.

<u>Sample answer</u>: When helping clients, you can do your best but not everyone will be happy all of the time. One client felt that I wasn't doing all I could to help and she came screaming into the office. I was able to calm the person down and she met with the president of our firm and was given the forum to complain. I had documented all of my work with this client and was able to show how I provided the same service here as I had to many happy clients. We had heard later that this client was dealing with other issues. It gave me the chance to strengthen my relationship with the president and explain my process of work.

Describe how you have persevered with a difficult problem in order to achieve a successful outcome.

<u>Why this question is being asked</u>: Every job has challenges and the interviewer likes to know how you handle them.

<u>Strategy</u>: Provide a relevant example of an incident that you encountered on the job, how you handled it and what was the end result.

<u>Sample answer</u>: In my first week on a job, I realized that data had not been tracked in an effective way for several years. There were paper files with some information and different online databases that contained other records. It was a mess. I wasn't sure how I'd dig myself out and even begin to focus on the job's main tasks. Thankfully, I had been working for a while at that point and had confidence that I could get things organized-eventually. I decided to speed up the process by coming in an hour early, working through lunch and staying an hour late to work on the organizing project, while I spent my regular work hours concentrating on the main aspects of the job.

What experience in your life has taught you the most?

<u>Why this question is being asked</u>: The interviewer wants to understand a part of what made you the person that you are.

<u>Strategy</u>: Focus on a particular challenge that you overcame and what you learned from it. If possible, discuss something that would be relevant to the job you are interviewing for.

<u>Sample answer</u>: Becoming a father has really helped to put my life in perspective. It has taught me to take a more serious approach to my personal life and helped me to focus better on my professional life as well. Time is the most important

commodity that we have and I try to maximize my time, both personally and professionally.

Who do you contact and communicate with on a regular basis, and for what purpose?

<u>Why this question is being asked</u>: Who you know and interact with is a reflection on you. The interviewer wants to know who makes up your network.

<u>Strategy</u>: Focus on your ability to maintain strong professional contacts throughout your career. Demonstrate that you are a professional that is always willing to take advice from others in order to learn.

<u>Sample answer</u>: Professionally, I am in regular contact with my first supervisor and my co-workers from that time. They were so generous in allowing me to learn from them and I often lean on them for advice. What has been especially rewarding is being in the position to assist them as well. I am glad not only to ask for help but be able to help as well.

What types of people do you get along with and why.

<u>Why this question is being asked</u>: Working in a job is often a collaborative experience. The interviewer wants to know what type of people you work with best.

<u>Strategy</u>: Provide examples that show you can get along with most people in any sort of environment.

<u>Sample answer</u>: The best types of people to work with are honest, open communicators who are willing to work together to achieve our objectives. I believe that I can get along with everybody, no matter what their background or experience level. Since my first job, I've worked with people

who were my age up to people in their senior years and we all got along great. I have respect for others and I am always willing to do what is needed to succeed.

What was the most traumatic experience to happen in your personal life?

<u>Why this question is being asked</u>: The interviewer wants to understand how you manage when times are difficult.

<u>Strategy</u>: Provide an experience that was difficult (such as the passing of a grandparent) without getting too personal. Focus your answer on how you dealt with the experience and were able to continue on with your life.

<u>Sample answer</u>: Thankfully, I haven't experienced a traumatic event that would fall outside of the regular circle of life. I was very close to my grandmother growing up and when she passed when I was 13, it was certainly difficult. It came at a time when I was transitioning from childhood to my teenage years and thinking of her helped to serve as a moral compass for me.

As I had to make difficult decisions, I would often think about what she would do in a similar situation and it made choices clearer for me.

When you go on vacation, when do you pack your suitcase?

<u>Why this question is being asked</u>: The interviewer wants to understand what type of planner you are.

<u>Strategy</u>: Avoid a brief answer such as the night before, a day before or a week before. Explain when you pack and why in a logical manner.

<u>Sample answer</u>: I definitely don't wait to do everything until the night before. I think about what I will need during the trip and what I want to use before I go. About a week before, I put in items that I know I won't need that week, such as my bathing suit if it is still winter in New York, but that I will use in Florida. I gather some of the clothes I plan to use but then I watch the weather forecast, just to make sure that it would be the best choice. The night before, I put in my essential items.

What do you consider yourself good at doing?

<u>Why this question is being asked</u>: The interviewer is trying to understand your greatest strengths as well as your confidence level.

<u>Strategy</u>: Provide examples of your abilities that would be relevant to your job. Focus on some things that you may not have been great at but you worked hard to improve.

<u>Sample answer</u>: I think I am a natural at listening to people and providing helpful advice. Other aspects of what I am good at didn't come easy, as I worked hard to learn them but now I think I am quite strong. Those skills include my spreadsheet knowledge, creating presentations and report writing.

On what do you spend your disposable income?

Why this question is being asked: The interviewer wants to know if you make sound decisions.

Strategy: Include information about some practical decisions that you make such as savings, investment and a college fund.

Sample answer: I put a certain percentage aside for a rainy day, put some towards investments and my daughter's college fund. I do take some time to relax and go out to restaurants and see a basketball game on occasion.

What's the most important thing you've learned in life?

Why this question is being asked: The interviewer wants to understand a part of what made you the person that you are.

Strategy: Provide an important lesson learned, how you came about learning it and why it is relevant to the job you are applying for.

Sample answer: No matter what situation you are in, you have to be true to your values. During my first week of a new job, I was asked to fabricate some records on behalf of the company. As I was counting on this job to support my family and solidify myself in the field, I began to do what I was told. I couldn't sleep and was stressed out about having to do this. I realized that it didn't fit my values no matter what the consequences. Thankfully, the company respected my wishes and I didn't have to participate in doing something like that. It reinforced for me that I would never do something that didn't fit my values, no matter what.

What is your greatest fear?

<u>Why this question is being asked</u>: The interviewer wants to gain greater insight into your personality.

<u>Strategy</u>: Explain the reason that you have a certain professional fear and how it relates to your job.

<u>Sample answer</u>: Professionally, it would be someone thinking that I am not doing my best. I have a very strong professional work ethic and give it all I have. I would be disappointed if someone put their trust in me and felt I was not doing my best.

Tell me about a problem you solved in a unique way. What was the outcome?

<u>Why this question is being asked</u>: Every job has problems that have to be solved and the interviewer wants to know how you have taken a unique approach to solving them in the past.

<u>Strategy</u>: Provide a problem facing your company that you helped to solve and the unique approach that you used. Describe something that would be relevant to the job you are applying for.

Sample answer: Due to some executive management mistakes in the past, my company had the perception of being a regionally based service provider. Since there was no budget to create an advertising campaign, I utilized my knowledge of social media to spread the word and gain traction in other markets. It was successful and the company now has accounts far outside of the region.

Tell me about a time when you made a decision without all the information you needed.

<u>Why this question is being asked</u>: Every job requires you to make judgment calls based on not having complete information. The interviewer wants to understand how you've handled it before in order to understand how you may handle it in the future.

<u>Strategy</u>: Provide an example of a decision you had to make that is relevant to the job you are applying for. Explain the whole process: What decision you had to make and why, how it turned out and what was the end result.

<u>Sample answer</u>: In the ecommerce space, we have to make predictions as to which items will be in demand for the holiday buying season. We look at historical sales figures and interest in products to prognosticate but it can be hard to know. Normally, it has worked out fine but some years it doesn't. The first couple of years I was involved, we took a hit but I was able to build in better metrics to look from our mistakes and improve for the future.

How frequent do you add contacts to your address book?

<u>Why this question is being asked</u>: Building connections and networking is an essential part of almost any business. The interviewer wants to understand how you establish and build your network.

<u>Strategy</u>: Explain how you build and nurture relationships effectively.

<u>Sample answer</u>: Every day. What's great about technology is that I can use a virtual address book or a networking site like LinkedIn to build my connections. Almost anyone is

appropriate to add, I just have to manage that new relationship effectively. I create categories to remind me of who this person is and keep notes to effectively manage the relationship and stay in touch to build the relationship.

Why is your current salary so high?

<u>Why this question is being asked</u>: Your salary may be out of the range that is normally paid for such a position and the interviewer would like to know how you secured that amount.

<u>Strategy</u>: Don't apologize for earning a higher salary than most. Prove that you are worth it, and more.

<u>Sample answer</u>: I performed many duties outside of my job title that allowed the company to save on costs. I am very accurate and work efficiently, which saves the company on additional costs. My boss knows that I am worth it and was glad to pay accordingly.

Why were you promoted?

<u>Why this question is being asked</u>: The interviewer would like to gain insight into how you were able to move up the corporate ladder.

<u>Strategy</u>: Discuss your accomplishments that lead to the promotion. Put a special focus on those accomplishments that would be relevant to the job.

<u>Sample answer</u>: I was promoted from account manager to trainer within one year. This was due to my stellar record of sales while maintaining and growing accounts as well as my ability to lead others and train them to work effectively.

What skills have you acquired from your internships?

<u>Why this question is being asked</u>: If you are a recent graduate with limited full-time work experience, the employer would like to learn what skills you can bring to a full-time position.

<u>Strategy</u>: Focus on skills gained from the internship that would be relevant to the job.

<u>Sample answer</u>: The most important skills that I learned were to manage my time, pay attention to detail and to work effectively in a team.

Tell me about a time when you had to give someone difficult feedback and how you managed it.

<u>Why this question is being asked</u>: In a management role, or otherwise, you may have to have a discussion with a co-worker or subordinate that is a difficult one. The interviewer wants to understand how you would manage it.

<u>Strategy</u>: Provide a relevant example that explains the situation leading up to the conversation, what was said during the conversation and what was the end result.

<u>Sample answer</u>: It is never easy to provide someone with difficult feedback but in order to work most effectively, you just have to do it sometime. A co-worker and friend seemed like his hygiene habits had dropped off significantly. He went from wearing sharp suits to stained shirts, seemed like he often skipped showers and stopped shaving. I had a private conversation with him and mentioned how others had noticed that his habits had changed and became concerned. He explained that he was overwhelmed with his wife recently having children and it hadn't been on his radar as much as it had in the past. He said that he would take care of it. He did change the way that he dressed and cleaned himself up. I am

glad that I told him as it probably would have cost him his job.

What skills have you acquired from your part-time jobs?

<u>Why this question is being asked</u>: If you are a recent graduate with limited full-time work experience, the employer would like to learn what skills you can bring to a full-time position.

<u>Strategy</u>: Focus on skills gained from the part-time job that would be relevant to the position.

<u>Sample answer</u>: As a waiter for a busy high-end restaurant, the most important skills that I learned were to manage my time, pay attention to detail and to work effectively in a team.

Do you think it is worthwhile to establish new relationships?

<u>Why this question is being asked</u>: Building connections and networking is an essential part of almost any business. The interviewer wants to understand how you establish and build your network.

<u>Strategy</u>: Explain why it is important to build and nurture relationships. Provide an example of how establishing a relationship has benefited you and your employer.

<u>Sample answer</u>: I believe that it is not only worthwhile but it is essential to build relationships. If you only lean on the relationships you had established in the past, your network is getting smaller everyday as people retire or move onto something else. With resources like LinkedIn, it is easier than ever to reach out and begin establishing new relationships. I have many examples but a quick email exchange with a wholesaler in Ireland helped to open up that market for our company.

How do you judge your own success?

<u>Why this question is being asked</u>: How you judge success will be telling of your ability to succeed. The interviewer wants to get insight into how successful you may be on the job.

<u>Strategy</u>: Provide insight into your self evaluation process. Share different ways of judging your success along the way. Provide an example or two that brings greater clarity to how you work.

<u>Sample answer</u>: I judge my success in many ways and at various intervals. Of course, how I meet or exceed various management set goals on the job is the most important- such as sales goals. But I set my own goals as well because it is important to know if I am on the right road. I like to look at various metrics along the way. What is my response rate on an advertising campaign? How many sales have I made at various intervals? And how many new relationships have been established?

What have you learned from your experiences outside the workplace?

<u>Why this question is being asked</u>: The interviewer wants to understand what you've learned outside the workplace that you can bring back to the job.

<u>Strategy</u>: Focus on a relevant skill or experience you have gained that would be helpful to the company. Give a story that explains what you've learned.

<u>Sample answer</u>: I enjoy volunteering to build homes for the less fortunate. It's given me the opportunity to take on project management skills- such as making a plan, maximizing resources and working with others.

4 WINNING INTERVIEW ANSWERS: YOUR EXPERIENCE

Why was there a gap in employment between [insert dates] and [insert date]?

<u>Why this question is being asked</u>: The interviewer wants to get a sense of your work ethic and is concerned about the gap in employment. He/she wants to know if you were let go and why.

<u>Strategy</u>: Even if the reason leading to an employment gap was not your decision, frame the answer in a positive sense. Explain what mistakes you may have learned from and how it will make you a better worker in the future.

<u>Sample answer</u>: Unfortunately, I was let go due to downsizing. I did enjoy my year and half at the company. It allowed me to learn more about the banking industry and demonstrate my skills. At the beginning, it was a little rough managing my time effectively but I improved vastly and I look forward to bringing my sharpened abilities to the next opportunity.

What have you learned from your experiences outside the classroom?

<u>Why this question is being asked</u>: For recent graduates, the interviewer would like to know what other experiences you have benefited from beyond textbook learning.

Strategy: Focus on what you learned from experiences that showed you were involved on campus and used your free time wisely.

Sample answer: After my first year, I worked as a volunteer tutor. It taught me to be patient and allowed me to become a better teacher. I was also in charge of the annual fundraiser for the athletics club. That taught me about teamwork, planning and especially budgeting.

What applicable experience do you have?

Why this question is being asked: The interviewer is most interested in a candidate who has excelled in a relevant role in the past as opposed to taking a risk on someone trying to learn a new role.

Strategy: As much as possible, try to make a direct connection between the roles you've held and the job you are interviewing for.

Sample answer: There are many similarities between my last job and this opportunity. Although they may be in different industries, the work processes are very similar. For example, I believe that the reporting of data milestones in an education environment are very similar as I had to…

Have you taught any courses?

Why this question is being asked: If the job requires instructing others, the interviewer would like to know if you have formal experience in a classroom setting.

Strategy: If you have experience teaching courses, discuss the aspects that would be relevant to this job.

Sample answer: Yes, I taught a few college courses on

communication in the past. It taught me to keep the material interesting and relevant to engage the audience. I still use these strategies when working with people of all different ages.

What did you dislike about your previous job?

<u>Why this question is being asked</u>: Not everything is going to go the way you expect on a job and the employer wants to understand how best you deal with it.

<u>Strategy</u>: Provide a negative that might be applicable to the previous job but you don't believe would be an issue in the job you are interviewing for. Also, explain how there might have been something you disliked but how you were able to work successfully regardless.

<u>Sample answer</u>: I normally don't focus on the negatives of a job as I believe it would be impossible to work in ideal conditions and part of a job is having the ability to be successful despite non ideal conditions. I am a team player and enjoy working in a collaborative environment. Management asked us to contact them whenever we finished an assignment as opposed to checking in with our co-workers and see if they needed help. Unfortunately, it slowed down the process and we weren't able to help each other effectively.

Have you ever had difficulty working with a manager?

<u>Why this question is being asked</u>: Conflict with management is a common occurrence and the interviewer wants to understand best how you can manage the conflict.

<u>Strategy</u>: Admit to a time that you had difficulty working with a manager and why and explain how you dealt with the

situation as well as the outcome.

<u>Sample answer</u>: After about two years at my first job I was assigned to report to a new manager. Her management style was very different from my previous supervisor's and it took some time to adjust. One manager was very hands on while the other was hands off, and each expected different ways of communication and reporting information. After a few miscommunications with the new manager, I asked for a meeting to clear the air by clarifying her expectations and preferences. It was very helpful and we actually ended up working very well together after that.

Have you given any presentations?

<u>Why this question is being asked</u>: As giving presentations is an important aspect of some jobs, the interviewer would like to learn more about your prior experience in this area.

<u>Strategy</u>: Discuss presentations that would be relevant to the job. Describe the material you presented and to what audience. Explain how the presentation was received.

<u>Sample answer</u>: Yes, I have been providing sales presentations for the last 7 years. For example, I provide a presentation on utilizing technology for sales people at the annual conference. There are usually 300 people in the audience. I always receive positive feedback.

Have you had experience firing people?

<u>Why this question is being asked</u>: If this is a function of the role, the interviewer wants to know if you have the stomach for it.

<u>Strategy</u>: If the answer is yes, provide insight into your

process for undertaking that action.

<u>Sample answer</u>: I have. It is never an easy process but in order for an organization to run efficiently, it has to be done sometimes. I am upfront with an employee when it is time as I don't want the person to feel uncertainty or allow for the possibility of rumors spreading as to the person's job status. It is important to provide feedback as to how he/she can improve in the future as well as provide resources so that he/she has a softer landing, such as outplacement services and a few weeks of severance pay.

What do you consider your most noteworthy accomplishment in your last job?

<u>Why this question is being asked</u>: To learn not only what you have done in a job but what you've actually accomplished.

<u>Strategy</u>: Provide an accomplishment related to the job you are interviewing for. Describe what needed to be done and how you went about doing it.

<u>Sample answer</u>: When I started in the position, there was a great deal of infighting amongst the employees. Multiple people wanted to claim credit for the same things. I didn't feel that this was a good environment for working together and meeting our goals. I spoke with each employee about the culture and how things got to be the way they are and looked to change things slowly. I thought communication was a key and encouraged people to get together and talk as opposed to making assumptions or just sending an angry email. I organized two retreats a year so that we can work on our team building skills. Most importantly I continued to reinforce that we all needed to work together for everyone to benefit.

Who was your worst boss?

<u>Why this question is being asked</u>: Conflict with management is a common occurrence and the interviewer wants to understand best how you can manage the conflict.

<u>Strategy</u>: Admit that you did have difficulty working with a manager and why and explain how you dealt with the situation as well as the outcome

<u>Sample answer</u>: Well, I wouldn't say that any boss was the "worst", as its natural for a manager and subordinate to have conflicts at times. But there was one who I thought would be my worst boss when we got off on the wrong foot. After about two years at my first job, I was assigned to report to a new manager. His management styles was very different from my first manager's, and it took some time to adjust. One manager was very hands on while the other was hands off, and each had different preferences for communicating and reporting information. After a few miscommunications with the new manager, I asked for a meeting to clear the air and go over his expectations and preferences. It was very helpful and we actually ended up working very well together after that.

Describe a time when you took extra effort to make sure the person with whom you were communicating with had really understood your point.

<u>Why this question is being asked</u>: To determine if you are a good communicator.

<u>Strategy</u>: Provide an example relevant to your job where you solicited feedback from somebody to learn if he/she understood what you were asking.

<u>Sample answer</u>: When I trained my sales team in some of the

new techniques that we would be using, I asked them to role play a sales call utilizing the techniques. It was helpful in determining if they understood what I was asking for.

Can you tell me about a situation, where you tried to solve a problem with ideas and methods that had not been tried before?

<u>Why this question is being asked</u>: To determine if you can use unique ideas to solve problems.

<u>Strategy</u>: Provide a relevant example that demonstrates how you used a unique idea to solve a problem.

<u>Sample answer</u>: Our company was known for having great products and customer service but unfortunately there was a glitch in using our software that was starting to hurt our business. Our client base was made up of many technically adept professionals who were complaining about this glitch. I decided that we should be transparent and admit that we've tried but can't seem to solve this problem. Via social media, we offered $10,000 to any of our "fans" who could figure out a solution. We had 3 people figure out the answer and divided up the monetary award. In addition to solving the problem, this unique approach also gave us positive publicity.

Can you tell me about a situation where you used your imaginative skills to solve a very difficult problem?

<u>Why this question is being asked</u>: To determine if you can use out of the box ideas to solve problems.

<u>Strategy</u>: Provide a relevant example that demonstrates how you used a unique idea to solve a problem.

<u>Sample answer</u>: Our company was known for having great products and customer service but unfortunately there was a glitch in using our software that was starting to hurt our business. Our client base was made up of many technically adept professionals who were complaining about this glitch. I decided that we should be transparent and admit that we've tried but can't seem to solve this problem. Via social media, we offered $10,000 to any of our "fans" who could figure out a solution. We had 3 people figure out the answer and divided up the monetary award. In addition to solving the problem, this unique approach also gave us positive publicity.

What could you have done to prevent a disappointing team experience?

<u>Why this question is being asked</u>: To learn how you can improve a situation when working with others.

<u>Strategy</u>: Explain the situation: what the objective was, why it didn't work and what could have been done to improve the end result.

<u>Sample answer</u>: A group of representatives from various departments were charged with creating an action plan to improve the organization's visibility in the market. It was difficult to get everyone on the same page or to even get together. When we did get together, we would get stuck on a

point without moving forward. To improve in the future, the team should break off into committees to tackle various issues before presenting it for consensus to the group. Once things are at a maturity stage, several dates can be proposed so that everyone can clear their calendars to come up with a working plan.

Did you receive any raises in your last job?

<u>Why this question is being asked</u>: To learn if you merited any raises from your last employer.

<u>Strategy</u>: If the answer is yes, explain what you accomplished in order to earn a raise.

<u>Sample answer</u>: I did. Every six months, there was a performance review. I consistently exceeded my sales goals and I was able to negotiate a raise bi-annually.

Describe a situation in which you dealt with a difficult customer.

<u>Why this question is being asked</u>: As handling difficult customers is a regular occurrence in many jobs, the interviewer wants to understand how you would best manage the situation.

<u>Strategy</u>: Provide some background into the situation before explaining how you handled the customer and what the end result was.

<u>Sample answer</u>: Our customer had ordered 100 copies of our art book to use as a giveaway for a fundraiser he was having. When he contacted us, the event was two days away and he was very disappointed to receive the black and white version of the book rather than the color. He explained that his budget had already been exhausted and he had promoted the

giveaway already. As I saw that the customer had been with us for years, I decided that it would be best for business long term if we overnighted 100 color copies and ate the cost. He was thrilled and it got us some great publicity in the nonprofit world plus a very loyal customer.

Tell me about a time when you disagreed with your boss.

Why this question is being asked: Conflict with management is a common occurrence and the interviewer wants to understand how you can manage the conflict.

Strategy: Admit that you did have difficulty working with a manager and why. Explain how you dealt with the situation as well as the outcome

Sample answer: As part of my role, I was asked to verify information with clients at various intervals, such as 90, 180 and 360 days. I was asked to complete my predecessor's reports. But I noticed that she must have been behind in her work because several verification dates had already passed. I did not accuse anyone of anything, but I contacted my supervisor to draw his attention to the problem. Since I had not been on the job for these past verification dates, I could not sign off to verify those communications. I said that I am a team player and would be willing to do whatever was necessary for the team, but that I could only verify information if I knew it to be true. The boss told me that he respected me for that and I was not asked again.

Describe a situation in which you were motivated to put forth your best effort.

<u>Why this question is being asked</u>: The interviewer wants to get a better sense of your work ethic and motivation.

<u>Strategy</u>: Make it clear that you have a strong ethic and are internally motivated.

<u>Sample answer</u>: The strongest motivation to put forth my best effort is the pride I have in myself as a professional. I am not satisfied until I have done my all. I also enjoy working in an environment where the co-workers motivate and push each other to succeed.

How did you acclimate to a major change in a role that you held?

<u>Why this question is being asked</u>: As change is constant in most jobs, the interviewer wants to know how you deal with it.

<u>Strategy</u>: Share an example from a past position that the interviewer would find relevant to the job you are interviewing for. Describe the situation, the change, why the change presented a problem for you and how you dealt with it.

<u>Sample answer</u>: The company policy had been to send sales people on the road 75-80% of the time during the year, which allowed us to interact well with potential clients and secure deals. The company slashed the budget for travel, which allowed for travel only half of the normal time. It presented a challenge as I thought that face to face meetings were the best way to sell. I began utilizing technology more, such as Skype and Gotomeeting, to create a connection with clients even if I couldn't meet them in person. It worked out very

well as less time on the road meant that I could spend more time pitching and I ended up selling more!

If your boss gives you a mountain of tasks at 3:00pm and says she needs them by 5:00pm, but you know you can't finish them in time, what do you do?

<u>Why this question is being asked</u>: The interviewer wants to know how you manage an unreasonable or unrealistic task.

<u>Strategy</u>: Provide a strategy that shows you are a team player and are willing to do whatever is necessary to try to achieve management's objective, but capable of providing a realistic viewpoint when it may be impossible to meet the objective.

<u>Sample answer</u>: I would tell my boss that I will clear my calendar for the rest of the day and I will do my best to complete as much of the work as possible. I would also provide insight that I do believe it will take longer than 2 hours to complete, and inquire if 5pm is a hard deadline. If it not, I would stay as late as necessary to complete it. If it was a hard deadline, I would ask the boss if I could ask my co-workers, who I know would be able to contribute as well, to drop what they are doing so that we can work on this together and complete by 5pm.

Tell me about the best boss you ever had.

<u>Why this question is being asked</u>: The interviewer wants to know what management style you would fit best with.

<u>Strategy</u>: Describe the best boss in a way that allows you to demonstrate your strongest skills and accomplishments.

<u>Sample answer</u>: I normally don't think of it as the best or worst boss as I can work with many different types of people

and under different management styles. I would say though that my last boss really played best to my strengths. I am a self-starter and my boss empowered me to take on additional responsibilities. I really grew into the job and my supervisor's confidence in me allowed me to excel. I also liked that his door was always open and no question was considered stupid. It allowed me to avoid any miscommunications or mistakes before they happened. He was quick to give praise but at the same time gave excellent constructive criticism.

Give an example of when you were faced with an obstacle completing an important project?

<u>Why this question is being asked</u>: As every task faces obstacles to completion, the interviewer wants to understand your process to overcome them.

<u>Strategy</u>: Provide a clear example of the type of obstacle you have encountered, what you did to manage it and the end result.

<u>Sample answer</u>: When faced with an obstacle, I consider all alternative paths to achieve the goal as well and strategize about how to remove the obstacle. For example, I am asked to plan our yearly conference. The most important step is to secure a venue and a date and then everything can follow after that. In reaching out to our usual venue, I was finding it difficult to secure a date as the weeks went by. I decided to seek out comparable venues, receive bids and plan all the steps that we would need to take for either venue. Once I had things set with the alternative spot, we moved forward with that venue. It turned out to be a great event.

Describe your latest written communications and how effective it has been.

<u>Why this question is being asked</u>: To gain more insight into your communication skills based on a recent example.

<u>Strategy</u>: Focus on the positive impacts of a recent communication such as a press release or an internal memo explaining an important issue.

<u>Sample answer</u>: There had been unfounded rumors that my employer was planning to lay off 20% of its workforce. Rather than writing a brief communication to try to squash a rumor, I wrote a longer communication explaining why it could not be true based on our current growth and our needs to continue to hire aggressively as opposed to laying people off.

Describe for me a situation in which you were proactive.

<u>Why this question is being asked</u>: Being proactive instead of reactive is an important trait that employers seek.

<u>Strategy</u>: Provide an example relevant to the position that showed how proactively benefited the employer.

<u>Sample answer</u>: My employer's business model was heavily reliant upon the European market. Even when our business remained strong during the financial crisis, I suggested that we pivot toward growing markets in India and Asia. This ended up helping us to grow in those fields and remove our exposure to losses in the European markets.

If you know your boss is 100% wrong about something, how would you handle it?

<u>Why this question is being asked</u>: The interviewer wants to understand how you would approach a sensitive topic with management while maintaining protocol.

<u>Strategy</u>: Explain how what you'd do would depend on the situation, with your respect for management being first and foremost.

<u>Sample answer</u>: How I would handle it would have to depend on the situation. If it is something inconsequential to my work with my boss and the bottom line of the company, I would have to consider how my boss would handle being told that he/she is wrong and possibly let it go. If it was something that might affect our productivity and the company's ability to meet its goals, I would ask to speak to my boss privately. I wouldn't want to tell him/her that the information was wrong in a meeting. I would explain that I trust his/her information but that in this case, I believe that he/she is wrong and why. I would leave it up to the boss to decide what to do with the situation.

Describe a situation where you did not agree with something your boss asked you to do and how you resolved the problem.

<u>Why this question is being asked</u>: Conflict with management is a common occurrence and the interviewer wants to understand how you can manage the conflict.

<u>Strategy</u>: Admit that you did have difficulty working with a manager and why. Explain how you dealt with the situation as well as the outcome

<u>Sample answer</u>: As part of my role, I was asked to verify

information with clients at various intervals, such as 90, 180 and 360 days. I was asked to complete my predecessor's reports. But I noticed that she must have been behind in her work because several verification dates had already passed. I did not accuse anyone of anything, but I contacted my supervisor to draw his attention to the problem. Since I had not been on the job for these past verification dates, I could not sign off to verify those communications. I said that I am a team player and would be willing to do whatever was necessary for the team, but that I could only verify information if I knew it to be true. The boss told me that he respected me for that and I was not asked again.

Why did you quit your job?

<u>Why this question is being asked</u>: The interviewer wants to understand what drove you to quit a job in the past to understand if that may or may not happen if you were to take a new job.

<u>Strategy</u>: Provide an explanation that focuses on why that situation was no longer working out for you, what you learned and why a new situation would be a better fit for you in the future.

<u>Sample answer</u>: I had been at my last job for four years. It was a great experience as I was able to be with the company as we grew from a team of four to twenty employees. I was given the opportunity to train others and serve in a team leadership role. As the industry took a downturn, the team dwindled down and my ability to use my new skills dwindled with it. I began interviewing for other positions before leaving but it became too difficult to attend multiple follow up interviews without it affecting my work on the job. I

decided to leave to concentrate fully on finding that next opportunity.

What experience do you have in this field?

<u>Why this question is being asked</u>: The interviewer is most interested in a candidate who has excelled in a relevant role in the past as opposed to taking a risk on someone trying to learn a new role.

<u>Strategy</u>: As much as possible, try to make a direct connection between the roles you've held and the job you are interviewing for.

<u>Sample answer</u>: There are many similarities between my last job and this opportunity. Although they may be in different industries, the work processes are very similar. For example, I believe that reporting of data milestones in an education environment are very similar as I had to...

What would your previous supervisor say your strongest point is?

<u>Why this question is being asked</u>: The interviewer wants to understand how your strengths match the job.

<u>Strategy</u>: Focus on a strength that would be especially valued on the job. Provide an example of how you used that strength successfully on the job.

<u>Sample answer</u>: My supervisor would say that my greatest strength is my can-do attitude. Someone can have all the skills in the world but if they aren't willing to give their all, every day at anytime for anybody, then those aren't great skills. I am always willing to do my best and help out as I know that it's all about meeting company bottom lines.

Tell me about the most boring job you've ever had.

Why this question is being asked: The interviewer wants to know what environment is, or more importantly is not, a good fit for you.

Strategy: Focus on a job whose core skill set was different from the job you are applying for. Explain how you maintained your professionalism and excelled despite the job not being as exciting as you expected.

Sample answer: My first job was data entry- all day, every day. I am more of a people person and it was boring. Despite finding the job boring, someone had confidence to give me the opportunity and I take a lot of pride in my work and I did my best. I ended up being the employee with the fastest speed and the most accuracy.

Have you been absent from work more than a few days in any previous position?

Why this question is being asked: The interviewer wants to know what type of work ethic that you have and the amount of time you show up helps to bring some clarity.

Strategy: If you haven't regularly taken off, explain the times that you did and why it was important. Provide some clarity into your strong work ethic.

Sample answer: I feel that when I am absent from a workday that I am missing out on something, so it is very rare that I take off at all. The only time I can recall being absent, with the exception of a vacation week during our slow time of year, was to help care for a family member after surgery.

Do you have the stomach to fire people?

<u>Why this question is being asked</u>: The interviewer wants to assess your ability to hold a management position and make difficult decisions.

<u>Strategy</u>: Prove that you can handle performing difficult responsibilities. Explain why you would be able to manage it.

<u>Sample answer</u>: Well, in this role I know that I would have to make some difficult decisions. It is a stomach churning experience to have to fire people. When it doesn't feel like that any longer, someone probably shouldn't be doing it. In the way I manage, I am looking for my company to run as effectively as possible. When we are doing that, we can help all of the employees at the company to support their families. From time to time, people no longer fit and we have to let them go in order to help the company to run as effectively as possible.

Why have you had so many jobs?

<u>Why this question is being asked</u>: The interviewer wants to know how long you'll remain on the job and is concerned about your past.

<u>Strategy</u>: Focus on why this job would be a fit for you long term and why you had to move jobs in order to advance yourself.

<u>Sample answer</u>: I have had to take risks to learn and advance myself in order to be in the position to compete for this job. Each opportunity was a great way for me to learn early in my career. I am now looking for a solid opportunity that I could grow in.

What's the most difficult part of being a (job title)?

<u>Why this question is being asked</u>: The interviewer wants to consider what difficult parts of your current job might be relevant to the position you are applying for.

<u>Strategy</u>: Focus on a difficulty that you deal with that would be relevant to the position you are applying for. Explain how you overcome the challenge.

<u>Sample answer</u>: It is a stomach churning experience to have to let people go. In the way I manage, I am looking for my company to run as effectively as possible. When we are doing that, we can help all of the employees at the company to support their families. From time to time, people no longer fit and we have to let them go in order to help the company to run as effectively as possible.

Can you describe a time when your work was criticized?

<u>Why this question is being asked</u>: The interviewer wants to understand how you deal with criticism.

<u>Strategy</u>: Admit that you have been criticized before, why you were and what you learned from the situation.

<u>Sample answer</u>: I was very enthusiastic to get my work done and I always wanted to finish it as quickly as possible. My boss noticed that I was handing in work a week or two before the actual deadline. While she did say that the work was strong, she suggested that I should take my time and do the best job possible. I took that to heart and now make use of all my time in order to do the best job.

Can you give me an example of your managerial skills?

<u>Why this question is being asked</u>: The interviewer wants to understand how you manage.

<u>Strategy</u>: Focus on a management skill that would be relevant for the job. Provide a story that would be memorable in demonstrating this skill.

<u>Sample answer</u>: My skill is in rallying my team to work together. I had learned of some infighting between team members. I asked the whole team to get together and discuss what issues we were having and smooth out any problems. We dealt with the miscommunication and discussed how we could work together to meet objectives. The team did get on board and we completed the project successfully.

Describe a situation in which you led a team.

<u>Why this question is being asked</u>: Leadership abilities are an important element of most jobs.

<u>Strategy</u>: Provide an example of your leadership abilities that would be relevant to the job you are applying for.

<u>Sample answer</u>: I was named the group leader for our expansion project. I was given the opportunity due to my history of meeting milestones and my ability to get along well with others. I really enjoyed the experience as I was able to train and support my peers. We all shined together as a team.

How did you handle a situation when the manager was unavailable?

<u>Why this question is being asked</u>: The interviewer wants to understand how you would handle a situation in the absence of a manager.

Strategy: Provide an example of a relevant issue that may occur and how you handled it successfully.

Sample answer: My supervisor has to give final approval to the production department before the presses can run. She was stuck on a tarmac overseas with limited internet connectivity and the deadline was approaching. I asked the production manager to tell me how late he could actually push the deadline and still finish the magazine on-time. We were able to push it a half an hour. To save additional time, I highlighted the main issues that I knew my boss would want to take an extra close look at before approval. She arrived with two hours to spare, reviewed the areas I highlighted and gave approval for the presses to roll!

Have you ever worked in a job that you hated?

Why this question is being asked: Not every job will be a great fit for everybody and the interviewer wants to get a sense of what situation was not the right fit for you.

Strategy: Although you are asked about something you "hated", don't be overly negative. Focus on why the situation may not have been ideal but you did your best to make it successful.

Sample answer: Well, I don't often think of hating any job as there are always positives and negatives to any situation. If I were to think about a job I didn't enjoy, it would be my first job in a call center. I consider myself a people person, someone who can think on my feet and who takes a creative approach to problem solving. The manager just wanted everyone to read from a script and not deviate so it wasn't a great fit for me. I was actually one of the most successful reps but I knew that the job wasn't for me.

What was your starting and ending rate of pay at your last position?

<u>Why this question is being asked</u>: The interviewer wants to get a sense of your expected pay rate based on your past history, as a salary negotiation tool.

<u>Strategy</u>: Make it clear that your past salary isn't necessarily reflective of your position in the market. Try to avoid extensive salary discussion before you are actually offered the job.

<u>Sample answer</u>: My starting salary was $56,000 and my ending salary was $73,000. I began at that salary as I was just transitioning into the industry and staying at the company allowed me to gain some great experience that I could utilize at a later point. I know that a salary of $73,000 is low for someone with my experience.

What is your salary history?

<u>Why this question is being asked</u>: The interviewer wants to get a sense of your expected pay rate based on your past history as a salary negotiation tool.

<u>Strategy</u>: Make it clear that your past salary isn't necessarily reflective of your position in the market. Try to avoid extensive salary discussion before you are actually offered the job.

<u>Sample answer</u>: For the first seven years of my career in social services, I started at $32,000 and finished at $47,000. When I transitioned to the corporate world, my starting salary was $56,000 and my ending salary was $73,000. I began at that salary as I was just transitioning into the industry and staying at the company allowed me to gain some great experience that I could utilize at a later point. I know that a salary of

$73,000 is low for someone with my experience.

Tell me about your most significant work experience.

<u>Why this question is being asked</u>: The interviewer wants to gain greater insight into your previous work experience to understand how you might do on a job in the future.

<u>Strategy</u>: Focus on a work experience that is relevant to the position you are applying for.

<u>Sample answer</u>: Similar to this position, I served as a process manager for five years. I oversaw the work of 7 employees. We reduced inefficiency by a 30% average each year.

Did you receive any promotions?

<u>Why this question is being asked</u>: The interviewer would like to look back on your history of achievement and advancement in order to properly gauge your potential for the future.

<u>Strategy</u>: If you do not have several examples, focus on one or two promotions that would be memorable for the interviewer to hear. Explain why you were deserving and what you accomplished when given the opportunity.

<u>Sample answer</u>: I was named the group leader for our expansion project. I was given the opportunity due to my history of meeting milestones and my ability to get along well with others. I really enjoyed the experience as I was able to train and support my peers. We all shined together as a team.

Which areas of your work are most often praised?

<u>Why this question is being asked</u>: The interviewer wants to hear about your strengths in order to consider how these

strengths would best match the job.

<u>Strategy</u>: Focus on two of your strengths that are most relevant to the job. Provide examples of when you were praised and why.

<u>Sample answer</u>: Management and clients have often praised me for two areas: my can-do attitude and my ability to work with everyone. For example, when our company was acquired we were asked to work with a similar unit at the acquiring company. It was quickly becoming a mess as everyone wanted to do things their own way. I volunteered to go work with the other unit and learn their processes and share what we did best with them as well, so that when we came back to the table we would all be on the same page and work more effectively together.

Which area of your work is most often criticized?

<u>Why this question is being asked</u>: The interviewer wants to hear about your weaknesses as to consider how they might affect your ability to perform on the job.

<u>Strategy</u>: Do admit that you have been criticized before. Provide an example of an area that would not adversely affect your ability to perform this job. Explain what you have learned or how you have improved following the criticism.

<u>Sample answer</u>: I am often ready to jump right into a project and get it done. I've been told to take a slower approach and make sure all bases are covered before I submit a project. I have taken this advice to heart as I've found that it is better to take it a bit more methodically and get it done right. I still work fast but now I double and triple check my work before it is submitted.

Do you take work home with you?

<u>Why this question is being asked</u>: The interviewer wants to know how seriously you take your work and what you are willing to do to complete it.

<u>Strategy</u>: Paint a picture of someone who is willing to do whatever is necessary to complete the work but not of a workaholic.

<u>Sample answer</u>: I do when it is necessary. I try to plan my schedule with my goals prioritized so that I can give myself enough time to complete everything before a deadline approaches. As that is not always possible, I try to come in early or work through lunch when necessary. If work still needs to get completed, I'll bring it on the train or work on it once my family has gone to sleep.

How many hours do you normally work?

<u>Why this question is being asked</u>: The interviewer wants to know how seriously you take your work and what you are willing to do to complete it.

<u>Strategy</u>: Paint a picture of someone who is willing to do whatever is necessary to complete the work but not of a workaholic.

<u>Sample answer</u>: Beyond the typical nine-to-five 40 hour work week, I put in as many hours as necessary to complete my work. During a quieter time of year, it may only be 40 or 45 hours a week. When it is our busier season, it may be 50-60, really depending on what needs to get done.

Tell me about the funniest role you have had on a job/project.

<u>Why this question is being asked</u>: The interviewer wants to get a sense of your personality by asking you what you find humorous.

<u>Strategy</u>: Be cautious of discussing something that may make it appear to the interviewer that you don't take your job seriously. Provide a story of a situation in which the position you were put in may have been humorous in hindsight.

<u>Sample answer</u>: Hmm, that is a good question as my role typical doesn't lend itself to funny or humorous situations. If I had to think of an example of something that was humorous in hindsight, it was when I was asked to substitute for my director at an executive meeting. The director was very cautious about someone else saying the wrong thing in a meeting and asked me not to say too much. Given that instruction, I had to respond to most questions with a generic answer or tell the executives at the meeting that I'd have to bring the questions back to my director and he'd respond to them.

Have you ever been given too heavy a workload?

<u>Why this question is being asked</u>: Many jobs have a heavy workload and the interviewer wants to understand how you best manage it.

<u>Strategy</u>: Discuss that you are often given more tasks than would be reasonable for one person to handle but how you are able to do so successfully.

<u>Sample answer</u>: In all of my roles, I was given a very heavy workload but that was ok. It gave me confidence that my supervisor felt I could handle it. It would have been overwhelming for many people but I am good at prioritizing

my time. I keep track of what has to be done when and adjust accordingly. I build in extra time for myself, such as shorter lunch breaks and coming in early, when I need to.

In what part-time job have you been most interested?

<u>Why this question is being asked</u>: The interviewer wants to get a sense of your work ethic and commitment to a job even when it is only part-time.

<u>Strategy</u>: Make it clear that you were serious about any job that you held. Focus on one which included experience relevant to the job you are applying for.

<u>Sample answer</u>: I found most part-time jobs that I held to be interesting as there was always something that I could learn. The job that I did find most interesting was working for a promotions street team. We were given sponsored promotional items, like pendants or t-shirts with a company logo, to distribute at busy commuting hubs in the city. We had to plan out the most effective times to distribute, where to position ourselves and how to grab someone's attention quickly. It was the kind of experience that you couldn't learn from a marketing textbook.

What do you consider the most important idea you contributed in your last job?

<u>Why this question is being asked</u>: The interviewer wants to understand what type of impact you can have on a job.

<u>Strategy</u>: Focus on an idea that would be relevant to the job you are applying for. Explain the reason you came up with the idea and what happened as a result.

<u>Sample answer</u>: My idea was to create one master database

where we could input all information as opposed to several reports with overlapping, and sometimes conflicting, information. Many of our departments were working on the same data and reporting in different ways and it was becoming a mess. I volunteered to become a project manager and work with the IT team to develop this database based on the needs of the departments.

Give me an example from a previous job where you've shown initiative.

<u>Why this question is being asked</u>: Going beyond your responsibilities and taking initiative is a valued trait and the interviewer is looking to learn if you possess that inclination.

<u>Strategy</u>: Provide an example of a time that you took initiative that would be relevant to the job you are seeking. Clearly explain the reasons you took the initiative, what you did and what it ended up accomplishing.

<u>Sample answer</u>: As our firm merged with a competitor, there was a lack of available employees to help train the staff that was newly acquired. I took the initiative to hold early am and lunch trainings to get them up to speed in things like using our database, communication protocols and sales processes.

Which of your specific skills acquired or used in previous jobs relate to this position?

<u>Why this question is being asked</u>: Lifelong learners are especially valued by employers and the interviewer wants to understand if you recently acquired new skills.

<u>Strategy</u>: Don't just list a skill. Also explain how you went about acquiring it, why you think it is valuable and how you used it.

<u>Sample answer</u>: I had moderate knowledge of Excel from previous jobs but I became an expert in running complex queries at my last job. I asked one of the IT professionals if I could shadow him during lunchtime as he worked on various reports. I was able to pick up a lot that way and I was able to supplement that by attending some formal trainings at work and watching training videos at home. I can now run complex reports, and that saves me literally days!

Whom may we contact for references?

<u>Why this question is being asked</u>: The interviewer wants to verify that what you have been saying is correct by finding people to vouch on your behalf.

<u>Strategy</u>: If you have a great relationship with your past supervisors, and have asked for permission to provide their information, they are your best references. If you didn't have a great relationship, instead provide people at the company who were in a senior capacity that can vouch for you.

<u>Sample answer</u>: I've brought a list of 5 references. The list includes past supervisors and senior people at the organization.

Can you provide references from your current or previous employer?

<u>Why this question is being asked</u>: The interviewer wants to verify that what you have been saying is correct by finding people to vouch on your behalf. The interviewer also wants to get a sense of the relationship you have/had with your last supervisor.

<u>Strategy</u>: If you have a great relationship with your past supervisors, and have asked for permission to provide their information, they work best as references. If you didn't have a great relationship, provide contact information for people at the company who were in a senior capacity that can vouch for you.

<u>Sample answer</u>: Since I am currently employed and my current supervisor does not know that I am interviewing, I would prefer not to list her. I do have three senior members of the team who do know that I am interviewing who would be happy to serve as references. I also have the names of my two previous supervisors, who have agreed to serve as references.

What motivates you to put forth your greatest effort?

<u>Why this question is being asked</u>: The interviewer wants to get a better sense of your work ethic and motivation.

<u>Strategy</u>: Make it clear that you have a strong ethic and are internally motivated. To add to that, give examples of motivators that would be relevant to the job.

<u>Sample answer</u>: The strongest motivation to put forth my best effort is the pride I have in myself as a professional. I am not satisfied until I have given my all. I also enjoy working in an environment where the co-workers motivate and push

each other to succeed.

Describe a contribution you have made to a team project you worked on.

<u>Why this question is being asked</u>: Many assignments are expected to be completed collaboratively and the interviewer wants to learn about how you can contribute.

<u>Strategy</u>: Provide an example of a project that would be relevant to the job you are applying for.

<u>Sample answer</u>: My team was responsible for creating a 360 degree competitor analysis report. I volunteered to do much of the heavy lifting in terms of data acquisition to allow my teammates to concentrate on further analyzing the information. I was also the person that gave the report its final polish and checked it for accuracy.

What was the name of your most recent employer?

<u>Why this question is being asked</u>: The interviewer wants to clarify conflicting information in the documents you submitted. Perhaps your resume listed one employer and you application listing something else as your most recent employment.

<u>Strategy</u>: Just provide accurate information and you should be fine. Clarify if necessary why there is a discrepancy in information.

<u>Sample answer</u>: My current employer is now called ABC Industries. Previously, they were known as The ABC Conglomerate, but changed the name in 2011.

Have you ever opted to resign from a position?

<u>Why this question is being asked</u>: The interviewer wants to understand what makes you unhappy in a job or what would make you want to leave.

<u>Strategy</u>: If you have left a job before, provide clarity as to why you left. Focus on the positives while you were there; explain what you learned and why you left to grow your career.

<u>Sample answer</u>: Yes. I was at my first job for 4 years. It was a great opportunity to learn more about the business. I had the opportunity to grow with my department and mentor others. During my final year there, there were many cutbacks and the workflow slowed. It seemed like a good time to take the skills that I had gained and move on.

Have you ever worked in a position where you felt you were not given enough to do?

<u>Why this question is being asked</u>: The interviewer wants to know how you make the best use of your time.

<u>Strategy</u>: Provide an example of completing your work early and how you made the best use of your time to benefit the company.

<u>Sample answer</u>: Yes, this has happened. In my last job, I became adept at processing my paperwork for the week by Wednesday. I would take the time to double check my work for accuracy but there was still plenty of time left. I spoke to my supervisor and asked if there was anything else that she needed me to work on. I volunteered to help my co-workers who might be seeking assistance.

How do you determine your priorities when you have multiple projects?

<u>Why this question is being asked</u>: Every job has multiple demands on your time and the interviewer wants to understand how you best manage.

<u>Strategy</u>: Explain your process and provide examples relevant to the job that demonstrate your ability to manage and prioritize multiple projects

<u>Sample answer</u>: To determine what must be prioritized I look at two things: when is it due and who is requesting it. I've found that executives expect you to drop everything and work on their projects as a first priority and that is what I normally do. Secondly, I look at the deadline and work on what is most pressing first. In my last job, I would get many requests from the CEO and would handle those first. To prioritize after that, I would look at what other work I had due and when. I would consider what was due in the distant future and how I could break up the work with an eye towards the long-term while meeting immediate deadlines.

Are you comfortable with strict deadlines?

<u>Why this question is being asked</u>: Most jobs have tight deadlines and the interviewer wants to know how you work in that type of environment.

<u>Strategy</u>: Answer with a resounding yes and provide examples of how you did so successfully in the past.

<u>Sample answer</u>: Yes. With today's constantly changing business world, you really have to be these days. I am great at prioritizing my time and can shift my priorities depending on what needs to be completed. In my last position, I was often called on to produce reports with little turn around time or advance notice. I put aside the other projects and

concentrated my time on meeting the deadline.

Do you check your messages while on vacation?

<u>Why this question is being asked</u>: The interviewer wants to know how well you maintain a work/life balance.

<u>Strategy</u>: Make it clear that you do stay in top of what is going on when you are away but that you are not a workaholic.

<u>Sample answer</u>: Doesn't everybody? Sometimes things come up that have to be taken care of before I return. I try to check my phone and email messages at least once a day and either respond or delegate someone else to take care of the matter until I return.

What is the worst job you can imagine holding?

<u>Why this question is being asked</u>: One job may be the perfect fit for one person and the worst fit for another. The interviewer wants to understand what type of job wouldn't be a fit for you.

<u>Strategy</u>: Choose a type of job that is very different from the one you are interviewing for. By showing what you don't want; make it clear what you do want.

<u>Sample answer</u>: Since I really enjoy working in the helping professions, any job that takes advantage of people would be the worst type I can imagine. An example that comes to mind would be someone signing people up for rapid refunds on their taxes when you know it is taking advantage of them.

Can you work without supervision?

<u>Why this question is being asked</u>: The interviewer wants to know what type of management style works best for you.

<u>Strategy</u>: Make it clear that you can work without supervision and provide a relevant example or two.

<u>Sample answer</u>: I can work under any management style including without supervision. Once it is clear what my objectives are and how the company wants me to execute those objectives, I can do the job. In my last position, the supervisor had responsibilities that pulled him in many different directions and he had little time to oversee my work. As I understood what was expected of me, I was able to work without a problem.

Give me an example of a time when you had to conform to a policy or rule that you did not agree with.

<u>Why this question is being asked</u>: The interviewer wants to know how you respond to a situation that you do not agree with.

<u>Strategy</u>: Provide an example relevant to the job that shows you were able to successfully conform to the policy.

<u>Sample answer</u>: When facilitating workshops, I was not allowed to let in attendees who came more than 10 minutes late. I knew that many of those who came late had prior family obligations and other issues to deal with that may have delayed them but I had to tell them about the policy and uphold it when they came late.

Describe a situation where your results have been below your

superiors' expectations.

Why this question is being asked: Not everything you do will be a success and the interviewer wants to understand how you dealt with a situation in which you were not successful.

Strategy: Provide a situation of inflated expectations relevant to the job that the interviewer would understand. Explain the steps that you took to try to meet expectations, what you accomplished and why it did not work out.

Sample answer: In 2011, I led a team of 12 sales agents in selling 10,000 widgets. In 2012, the company asked our department to sell 12,000 widgets despite having a 25% reduction in staff. We were able to do more with less, as I trained the agents in maximizing their time and efficiency by utilizing more technology tools in reaching out to clients and we were able to sell 10,500 widgets in the end. I thought this was a tremendous accomplishment for our team to beat last year's total with fewer staff members but it was below my superiors' expectations so that was a disappointment.

How did you adapt to a major change that occurred in a job that you held?

Why this question is being asked: As change is constant in most jobs, the interviewer wants to know how you deal with it.

Strategy: Share an example from a past job that the interviewer would find relevant to the job you are interviewing for. Describe what the situation was, what change was implemented, why the change presented a problem for you and how you dealt with it.

Sample answer: The company policy had been to send sales

people on the road 75-80% of the time during the year, which allowed us to interact well with potential clients and secure deals. The company slashed the budget for travel, which allowed for travel only half of the time. It presented a challenge as I thought of face to face meetings as the best way to sell. I began utilizing technology more, such as Skype and GoToMeeting, to create a connection with clients even if I was not there. It worked out very well as less time on the road meant that I could spend more time pitching and I ended up selling more!

What are the steps you follow to study a problem before making a decision?

<u>Why this question is being asked</u>: There are always challenges on the job and the employer wants to understand how you manage them.

<u>Strategy</u>: Provide an example relevant to the job that proves your ability to diagnose the problem, consider the possibilities and make the best decision.

<u>Sample answer</u>: No matter what the problem, I've found that the most important things are to stay calm and not to make any irrational decisions. My process is usually the following: Once a problem has been identified, I diagnose the cause of the problem, find the right people to fix it and then ensure the problem is fixed. We had an issue where it seemed like our database had lost about a third of the essential data. Our team tried several different ways to retrieve the information and made note of exactly what was missing. Once I determined that it was out of our scope of comprehension, I worked with the IT team to recover the information and make sure that it was in running order. We could have

panicked or spent weeks inputting the information again but this ended up as the best way to go.

What was the most important task you ever had?

<u>Why this question is being asked</u>: The interviewer wants to determine how you handle responsibility.

<u>Strategy</u>: Provide an example of a task that you handled that is relevant to the job and shows your ability to lead. Be sure to include what you accomplished.

<u>Sample answer</u>: My firm gave me the responsibility of coordinating our volunteer efforts. Each member of our team is tasked with volunteering 100 hours each year. We had so much talent to work with that I didn't want their efforts to be wasted by working in a role that did not suit them. I reached out to 50 local non-profits and asked them to send me lists with descriptions of what volunteer opportunities they most needed to fill. I then met with my co-workers to determine what type of experience they were looking for to make the best match possible. It worked out great! Most people really enjoyed the volunteer experience and our CEO is thinking of expanding the volunteer hours next year as he feels that it improves office moral and when employers return to work, they are more productive.

How do you get a peer or colleague to accept one of your ideas?

<u>Why this question is being asked</u>: Getting a co-worker excited about your idea is an important aspect of working effectively in a team.

<u>Strategy</u>: Explain your process of getting a colleague on board with your ideas and provide an example relevant to the job.

<u>Sample answer</u>: The most important thing is to listen to the ideas of others first. Once you know what a colleague wants to accomplish or get out of a project, it is helpful to incorporate their suggestions into your pitch. In my last position, my teammates and I were tasked with creating more effective recruitment techniques. I asked each team member what ideas they had and what they thought was important. When I presented my ideas, I made sure to acknowledge their objectives were for the project and how they could all work together.

Have you given any seminars?

<u>Why this question is being asked</u>: Presenting your ideas in a public forum will be an aspect of the job and the interviewer would like to learn about your relevant experience.

<u>Strategy</u>: If you have, provide examples of what you presented, how you prepared and how the audience responded to the material. If you haven't done a formal presentation in a work setting before, it is ok to draw an example from another aspect of life.

<u>Sample answer</u>: I gave a two-part seminar at our annual industry conference for the last five years. I believe that you cannot be over prepared and I practice many times and try to prepare for any eventualities. If appropriate, I add in as many interactive elements as possible to keep the audience engaged. I've always gotten positive feedback and I've been asked by audience members to speak at their events.

How did you get your last job?

<u>Why this question is being asked</u>: The interviewer may want to know how you sold the interviewer based on your limited experience for the role.

<u>Strategy</u>: Focus on the elements of securing the job that would be most of interest to the employer. If you got your last job because the place was owned by your cousin, you don't have to emphasize that.

<u>Sample answer</u>: My former supervisor identified me as an appropriate candidate when he heard of an opening at his new employer. Although I hadn't previously worked in a capacity similar to that of the open position, management was impressed with my history of accomplishment in other fields and potential to be a quick learner.

How does your present position differ from past ones?

<u>Why this question is being asked</u>: The interviewer wants to understand if you've grown in your career or stood still.

<u>Strategy</u>: Focus on the additional responsibilities you've taken on and how you've grown.

<u>Sample answer</u>: My present position has been a great opportunity to utilize all of the knowledge that I've acquired in the past. I have taken on the additional responsibility of becoming a team leader, the first time that I've been in a management role.

Why are you dissatisfied with your present job?

<u>Why this question is being asked</u>: The interviewer wants to know why you want to leave in order to consider if this job would be a better fit for you.

<u>Strategy</u>: Focus on the positive reasons for change and avoid

any negative reasons. Explain why you are looking to grow and seeking the next step.

Sample answer: Thankfully, I am not dissatisfied as I work with a great team but I am looking to explore my options. The opportunities for growth at my present employer are limited and I want to see where my skills would fit best and what possibilities are out there now that I've been in the field for twelve years.

What would your current employer have to do to convince you to stay there?

Why this question is being asked: The interviewer wants to understand how happy or unhappy you are in the job and gain further clarity into the situation.

Strategy: Focus on the positive and avoid any negativity. Explain why you are looking to grow and seeking the next step.

Sample answer: My current employer has really done so much for me that it isn't a case of what they would have to do for me to stay, but rather that I am now looking to grow and take on more responsibility than they can offer. My current employer has a small structure and to grow I really need to move on.

How did your last job influence your career?

Why this question is being asked: The interviewer wants to understand how you learn from each situation and what influence that has had on you now.

Strategy: Focus on aspects of what you've learned that would be helpful to the job you are interviewing for. Provide relevant examples to back up what you are explaining.

Sample answer: My last job allowed me to take on more management responsibilities and that has influenced my ability to take on a full-time role as a manager. I was able to lead a team under tight deadlines to exceed management expectations.

Are you currently under any employment contract obligation with current or previous employers?

Why this question is being asked: The interviewer wants to know your work status and if there are any issues that have to be navigated in order to sign a contract.

Strategy: Assuming that you are free to move on, make it clear that the only issue is non disclosure of company information and you will respect that.

Sample answer: I am work for hire so I am under no specific obligation. It would be appropriate to give two weeks notice. I'd like to give three if possible. The only other issue I can think of is non disclosure of company information. Which of course, I would respect to the fullest.

Recall a time from your work experience when your supervisor was unavailable and a problem arose.

Why this question is being asked: The interviewer wants to understand how you would handle a situation in the absence of a manager.

Strategy: Provide an example of a relevant issue that may occur and how you handled it successfully.

Sample answer: My supervisor has to give final approval to the production department before the presses can run. She was stuck on a tarmac overseas with limited internet connectivity and the deadline was approaching. I asked the production manager to tell me how late he could actually push the deadline and still finish the magazine on time. We were able to push it a half an hour. To save additional time, I highlighted the main issues with editorial that I knew my boss would want to take an extra close look at before approval. She arrived with two hours to spare, reviewed the areas I highlighted and gave approval for the presses to roll!

How do you organize the work you need to do when you have to handle multiple responsibilities?

<u>Why this question is being asked</u>: Every job has multiple demands on your time and the interviewer wants to understand how you best manage.

<u>Strategy</u>: Explain your process and provide examples relevant to the job that demonstrate your ability to manage and prioritize multiple projects

<u>Sample answer</u>: To determine what must be prioritized I look at two things: when is it due and who is requesting it. I've found that executives expect you to drop everything and work on their projects as a first priority and that is what I normally do. Secondly, I look at the deadlines and work on what is most pressing first. In my last job, I would get many requests from the CEO and would handle those first. I would examine what other work I had due and when. I would consider what was due in the distant future and how I could break up the work over time while working on what is due immediately.

What skills have you acquired from your work experience?

<u>Why this question is being asked</u>: The interviewer wants to get a better sense of your skills as well as how you've acquired them.

<u>Strategy</u>: Provide examples that show strong technical know how relevant to the job as well as how you've improved your soft skills through your work experience.

<u>Sample answer</u>: Many of the things that I learned in the classroom for this industry I did not become skilled in until I applied them on the job and learned from the expertise of others. In addition to my strong technical know-how in this industry, the most important skills that I learned were the importance of being a team player and being able to work with all different types of personalities to meet company objectives.

When given an important assignment, how do you approach it?

<u>Why this question is being asked</u>: Every job has important assignments and the interviewer wants to understand how you best handle that situation.

<u>Strategy</u>: Provide an explanation of how you prioritize the assignment, focus on the task and meet the objectives.

<u>Sample answer</u>: When I receive a priority assignment, I first look at my other responsibilities and determine how I can best clear my plate in order to focus on the priority work. I then make sure that I clearly understand the assignment and will ask for clarity from a supervisor, if necessary. I'll make sure I have the right resources in order to do the work and gather those resources if I don't have them, whether it be co-workers or technology. I'll prioritize the assignment until it is complete and request constructive criticism from my

supervisor, so that I can improve for next time.

Have you ever been asked to leave a position?

<u>Why this question is being asked</u>: The interviewer wants to understand why a job did not work out in the past.

<u>Strategy</u>: Assuming that you have been let go from a job, focus on what you've learned from a negative outcome and how you are a better employee today.

<u>Sample answer</u>: Yes. I worked in my first job for one year. At the one year evaluation, my contract was not renewed. Rather than deny that I had made any mistakes, I asked my supervisor for a candid evaluation of what I had done right but more importantly where things had gone wrong. It was very helpful for me to learn and grow as a professional. I became more aware that I had to ask more questions, not focus on the clock but make sure that the work was resolved before I left and how to become a better co-worker. When I think back on the type of employee that I was in my first job, it is kind of embarrassing as I was doing my best at the time but it is rewarding to know how much I've grown since then.

What percentage of your time is spent on each of your job responsibilities?

<u>Why this question is being asked</u>: The interviewer wants to understand how you best manage your time.

<u>Strategy</u>: Focus on your ability to be flexible and best manage your priorities.

<u>Sample answer</u>: I focus my time based on what the current priorities and deadlines are for the company. When it is selling season, I may focus 70% of my time on meeting with

clients and only 30% on report writing. When it is a quieter season, such as around the holidays, the prioritization would be reversed.

What social obligations go along with a job in this field?

<u>Why this question is being asked</u>: The interviewer wants to know if you understand the business and demands on your time outside traditional hours.

<u>Strategy</u>: Demonstrate your knowledge of the social obligations required outside the 9 to 5.

<u>Sample answer</u>: I know that social situations are a great way to network and there are many opportunities to grow business by attending regular local meet ups and the occasional regional convention. I am ready to commit to these types of events as I know that they are crucial to success.

In what ways does this type of work interest you?

<u>Why this question is being asked</u>: The interviewer wants to understand what makes you passionate about this field.

<u>Strategy</u>: Show your passion for the field and why it is a great fit for you.

<u>Sample answer</u>: I've always enjoyed helping others and when I learned about what social workers do, I knew that it would be a great fit for me. Working in the field for the last ten years has grounded me in the challenges of the field but that doesn't make me love it any less.

Do you participate in many social activities with your co-workers?

<u>Why this question is being asked</u>: The interviewer wants to

understand what type of team player you are and your balance of work/life.

Strategy: Demonstrate that you are a team player and know that it is important to participate in order to build a good rapport but that you have to balance it with your personal life as well.

Sample answer: I do participate in some. It is a good opportunity to get to know co-workers outside of a work situation. I wouldn't say that I participate in many but we do go out regularly, about once a month.

What did you like most about the kind of jobs you held in the past?

Why this question is being asked: To understand what type of work gives you satisfaction and why.

Strategy: Focus on the progressive nature of each opportunity. Give examples that would be relevant to this job.

Sample answer: The thing that I enjoyed most about the jobs I've held in the past is the opportunity to take on additional responsibilities as I learned. For example, in my first job I learned the business and within two years, I was training others.

When were you happy at work?

Why this question is being asked: To understand what makes you happy on a job.

Strategy: Paint an overall positive picture of a happy employee in most situations. Provide examples of what made you happy that would be relevant to the job.

Sample answer: I am happy most of the time at work. I enjoy working in this field and being challenged. I am most satisfied when I am helping my co-workers to succeed.

Describe a task you have done recently for which you exerted a high level of effort.

Why this question is being asked: To understand your work ethic and how/when you apply it on the job.

Strategy: Provide an example that would be relevant to the job you are applying for. Explain why it was necessary to exert the effort, how you went about the task and what you accomplished.

Sample answer: My firm transitioned into a new database recently but it was not properly tested. Many employees were reporting that data was missing. I took on the responsibility of fully investigating what happened. I documented all of the cases of missing data and worked with the IT department to recover the information and understand how we could avoid something like this happening again. This was outside of my regular work responsibilities so I spent a lot of late nights and early mornings at the office. My database is now running smoothly and no one is reporting missing any information.

Given a choice in your work, what do you like to do first?

Why this question is being asked: To understand how you manage your time.

Strategy: Demonstrate that you are good at managing and prioritizing your time. Provide an example of how you do so that is relevant to the job.

Sample answer: If there is not a priority deadline, I like to tackle the most challenging assignment first. When I do that, it gives me less time to worry and more time to prepare. I like to begin working on the year end report in August so that everything is in order by December.

Given a choice, which kind of task would you leave for last in your work?

<u>Why this question is being asked</u>: To understand how you manage your time.

<u>Strategy</u>: Demonstrate that you are good at managing and prioritizing your time. Provide an example of how you do so that is relevant to the job.

<u>Sample answer</u>: If there is not a priority deadline, I like to leave the assignment that I am most comfortable handling for last. By the time I get to it, I have already completed my most difficult assignments. Although it was challenging at first, I am proficient at running comparison reports and analysis for the company so I am comfortable leaving that for last.

When you are on vacation, what do you miss most about your work?

<u>Why this question is being asked</u>: To see how you will describe your job when you are on a break.

<u>Strategy</u>: Be positive but be careful to avoid seeming disingenuous. You won't be taken seriously if you say you miss absolutely everything. Provide one example that would be relevant to the job you are interviewing for.

<u>Sample answer</u>: Although it is a demanding environment, I get used to the hustle and bustle of the work week and I do miss it, somewhat, when I am away. My vacations are usually just a few short days here and there so thankfully I don't have

to miss work too much.

Why were you transferred?

<u>Why this question is being asked</u>: To understand if the reason you were transferred was a positive or negative one.

<u>Strategy</u>: Focus on the positives of the transfer, no matter what happened.

<u>Sample answer</u>: I was transferred during a time of much reshuffling at the company. It was a great opportunity for me to take what I had learned in one division and apply it to another.

Given the achievements on your resume, why is your salary so low?

<u>Why this question is being asked</u>: The interviewer wants to understand how much the salary factors in to your career goals.

<u>Strategy</u>: Explain your long term strategy in preparing yourself for the highest future earnings as opposed to taking whatever highest paying job comes next.

<u>Sample answer</u>: Up to this point in my career, it has all been about contributing to the organization and getting as much experience as possible. I chose to take some jobs that paid in the middle range of the market as opposed to the highest, as I knew those firms would challenge me the most and I'd have the best opportunity to learn. Now that I've gained all of that experience, I feel that I am in the position to pursue a job that adequately meets both of my goals- to challenge me as well as pay a salary that is at the higher end of the scale.

How does this job fit into your career plan?

<u>Why this question is being asked</u>: To understand if this position is a good fit for you or if it is just a job.

<u>Strategy</u>: Using your past experience and explaining your career goals, describe why this job is a perfect fit for you.

<u>Sample answer</u>: My goal has always been to take on roles of increasing responsibility in the advertising industry. I worked my way up from coordinator, to junior account rep. to Account rep. This job as an Account Manager is the perfect opportunity for me to take that next step and prove myself.

At your last internship, what tasks did you spend most of your time on?

<u>Why this question is being asked</u>: To understand if the internship listed on your resume was a valuable experience or just busy work.

<u>Strategy</u>: Provide examples that show the work you participated in was meaningful and that it was a worthwhile experience.

<u>Sample answer</u>: In my last internship, I supported the vice president of marketing. It was a unique opportunity as the company was emerging from bankruptcy and was short staffed. I took on some roles that I had not expected to have an opportunity to participate in as an intern: I provided competitive market analysis, prepared reports and presentations and accompanied the vice president to conferences. It didn't feel like the busy work that most internships are known for.

Can you tell me about a time when you discovered a more efficient way to do a work task?

<u>Why this question is being asked</u>: To understand if you look to improve your efficiency as a worker.

<u>Strategy</u>: Provide an example that would be relevant to the job you are interviewing for. Describe the challenge, how you went about solving it and what the end result was.

<u>Sample answer</u>: I was tracking vast amounts of data on spreadsheets. At certain times, I was doing a manual count of information on the spreadsheet but I knew there had to be a better way. On my own time, I started doing online tutorials to improve my knowledge of the program and I learned how to sort and review data more efficiently. It was like night and day. Something that had taken me about 5 or 6 hours to do, now took 1 or 2 hours.

Do you always double-check your work?

<u>Why this question is being asked</u>: To understand how meticulous you are in your work and how you minimize errors.

<u>Strategy</u>: Demonstrate that you are careful about checking your work but aware of time constraints as well. Mention any techniques you use that reduce errors in a time saving manner.

<u>Sample answer</u>: I am very meticulous and careful about my work. If it is a new process for me or something I am not yet confident in, I will double and sometimes even triple check my work. If it is a task that I am very comfortable with, I will spot check for errors.

Tell me about a time when you were given an assignment, but you were not clear on how to go about it. How did you tackle this situation?

<u>Why this question is being asked</u>: To understand how you would proceed when your directives are uncertain.

<u>Strategy</u>: Show that you are careful about understanding what is required of you and that you are not above asking for clarity or help when it is needed.

<u>Sample answer</u>: I was asked to produce the year end report that would be provided to our board of directors. It was not clear in what format this was expected to be delivered. I reviewed the directives to make sure I understood them and prepared some basic outlines so I had some visuals when requesting a meeting for clarity with my boss. I requested a meeting and brought in my materials. I explained the assignment as I understood it and requested clarity. The boss found it helpful that I had drawn up some mockups and explained to me exactly how he wanted it done.

Can you tell me about a time when you backed off in a meeting because you felt someone else should speak or have an opportunity?

<u>Why this question is being asked</u>: To understand how ego driven you are and how you best interact with co-workers or clients.

<u>Strategy</u>: Demonstrate your ability to champion a point but not to the extent of stepping over others in a meeting or being egotistical. Use an example that would be relevant to the job you are applying for.

<u>Sample answer</u>: When I was a junior employee, I was asked to sit in on a planning meeting and share my thoughts for reaching a new demographic. As a new employee, I was given the floor first and championed my cause. There were some senior employees who disagreed with my viewpoints based

on their years of experience and took the spotlight. I felt that it was the best I could do given the hierarchy at the time and that the CEO had heard my point and could make a decision for herself.

How would you show co-workers the importance of cooperation?

<u>Why this question is being asked</u>: Being able to work effectively with co-workers is an essential tool.

<u>Strategy</u>: Use an example relevant to the job that demonstrates your ability to get co-workers on the same team.

<u>Sample answer</u>: I am a data driven person and I would create a chart that compares what we can do separately compared to what we could accomplish together to meet objectives. It is hard to think outside of ourselves, but when a person sees a visual of how he/she can work most effectively in a group, it is memorable.

Give an example of a time when you assisted a co-worker to enhance their work skills?

<u>Why this question is being asked</u>: To understand if you are helpful to your co-workers.

<u>Strategy</u>: Provide an example relevant to the job that demonstrates how you helped a co-worker to learn that skill. Explain what difficulty your co-worker was having, how you went about assisting him or her and what the end result was.

<u>Sample answer</u>: One of my co-workers is an excellent salesperson but her computer skills were out of date. She was finding that her inability to run reports in a database was cutting into her time to call clients. I asked Sally to shadow me for a few days while I entered reports and to take notes of what she did not understand. I was able to go over her questions with her and watch while she entered some information as well to see if she was doing it correctly. I corrected some minor errors and Sally was off and running. She is now very capable in using the program and it is no longer a problem for her.

Tell me about a situation in which you were given job instructions and you were unable to comprehend the instructions.

<u>Why this question is being asked</u>: To understand how you would proceed when your directives are uncertain.

<u>Strategy</u>: Show that you are careful about understanding what is required of you and that you are not above asking for clarity or help when it is needed.

<u>Sample answer</u>: I was asked to produce the year end report that would be provided to our board of directors. It was not clear in what format this was expected to be delivered. I

reviewed the directives to make sure I understood them and prepared some basic outlines so I had some visuals when requesting a meeting for clarity with my boss. I requested a meeting and brought in my materials. I explained the assignment as I understood it and requested clarity. The boss found it helpful that I had drawn up some mockups and explained to me exactly how he wanted it done.

How often do you discuss and work with colleagues to think up new systems and styles of working?

Why this question is being asked: To learn if you are an innovative thinker looking to improve.

Strategy: Demonstrate that you do have discussions on how you can all work more effectively. Provide an example of a time that it proved effective.

Sample answer: My colleagues and I are constantly sharing best practices for how we can work most effectively. Whether it is process or technology related, we are always looking for ways to improve. I've found that a lot of innovation takes place informally during lunch time or the ride home where we can share what is working and what can be improved.

Can you tell me about a time when you did something extra, something not part of the routine activities assigned to you, for the benefit of the customer?

Why this question is being asked: To learn if you are the type of employee who goes above and beyond for the customer.

Strategy: Provide an example relevant to the job that clearly explains what extra step you took to help the customer. Explain why you were looking to help, what type of help you provided and what the end result was.

<u>Sample answer</u>: When I was covering our customer service line, I received a call from a longtime customer who was having difficulty accessing the information over the website. He was older and not proficient in navigating the internet. I inquired if he had access to a fax machine. He responded that he did and I faxed him the information, confirmed that he got it and reviewed the steps necessary to make his order. He was so happy to receive the help that he ended up ordering 20% more than usual.

Describe a time when you took on additional work to help your team meet a crucial work goal?

<u>Why this question is being asked</u>: To learn if you are the type of employee who will go the extra mile to help out your co-workers.

<u>Strategy</u>: Provide a relevant example that explains why it was necessary to take on the assignment, what you did to help and what the end result was.

<u>Sample answer</u>: Our team was working towards meeting the deadline for the end of year report. I had completed the analysis part but my team needed help with making the data visually appealing. I volunteered to polish up each image as it came in to make the presentation look its best.

Tell me about a time that you undertook a course of study, on your own initiative, in order to improve your work performance?

Why this question is being asked: To understand your motivation to keep learning and improving.

Strategy: Draw on an example of a formal or informal learning process that made you better at your job. Explain how you have improved.

Sample answer: My knowledge of Microsoft Excel was sufficient to get by but I wanted to become more effective at my work. I started doing advanced tutorials during my lunchtime to improve. Within a month, my knowledge vastly improved. I am now able to apply functions that improve my efficiency and save time.

Tell me about an initiative you have taken to improve procedures at work.

Why this question is being asked: Organizations value employees who take initiative and are helpful in improving the way things run.

Strategy: Provide a relevant example that explains what the problem was, the initiative that you took and the end result.

Sample answer: I noticed that the same information was being entered in multiple places at my company. I inquired if there was any good reason for this and I was told that there wasn't. I worked with the IT team to create a database that would encompass all of the required formats and fields of entry so that the information could be entered once and save time. We worked together on this for six months and now the company has just one database.

When you need to create an order of job tasks that need to be completed, how do you decide which task has priority?

<u>Why this question is being asked</u>: Every job has multiple demands on your time and the interviewer wants to understand how you best manage.

<u>Strategy</u>: Explain your process and provide examples relevant to the job that demonstrate your ability to manage and prioritize multiple projects.

<u>Sample answer</u>: To determine what must be prioritized I look at when work is due and who is requesting it. I've found that executives expect you to drop everything and work on their projects as a first priority and that is what I normally do. Secondly, I look at the deadline and work on what is most pressing first. In my last job, I would get many requests from the CEO and would handle those first. I would look at what other work I had due and when. I would consider what was due in the distant future and how I could break up the work over time while working on what is due immediately.

When was the last time you used an inventive method to draw out company resources beyond a level that is usually met?

<u>Why this question is being asked</u>: To understand your ability to maximize resources and save the company money.

<u>Strategy</u>: Provide a relevant example that demonstrates your ability to maximize resources in a creative way.

<u>Sample answer</u>: As part of our consulting work, we provide vocational testing. Each official test costs $50 and we normally purchase 2,000 per year. I had noticed that some clients take the first part of the test and do not complete it. Rather than waste the test on those who aren't going to

actually use it, I found a valid free version online. It is less comprehensive but it shows us who is serious about taking the exam. Once someone completes the free version, we administer the one that costs $50.

Explain how your work experience is relevant to this position.

<u>Why this question is being asked</u>: To understand your relevant experience for the position.

<u>Strategy</u>: Focus on the aspects of your experience that are most relevant to the position, whether you have had the actual job title before or not.

<u>Sample answer</u>: All of my professional experience has relevance to this sales manager opportunity. In my sales and account manager roles I've taken on increased responsibility. I've also managed others in retail and food services environments, which has taught me to be a better manager.

What relevant experience do you have?

<u>Why this question is being asked</u>: To understand your relevant experience for the position.

<u>Strategy</u>: Focus on the aspects of your experience that are most relevant to the position, whether you have held the actual job title before or not.

<u>Sample answer</u>: All of my professional experience has relevance to this sales manager opportunity. In my sales and account manager roles I've taken on increased responsibility. I've also managed others in retail and food services environments, which has taught me to be a better manager.

Could you have done better in your last job?

<u>Why this question is being asked</u>: To understand how you evaluate yourself and when you see room for improvement.

<u>Strategy</u>: Don't be too hard on yourself. Emphasize what you did right but what in hindsight, could have been done better.

<u>Sample answer</u>: There is always room for improvement. I did have a consistently strong track record of being the highest producer of sales in the company but at times I should have put my focus on different markets. For example, I initiated some contracts in the education market but that industry tends to move very slowly and it affected my ability to build new business in technology. If I'd have researched it better, I'd have put more of my focus on technology and stuck with only the major accounts in education.

5 WINNING INTERVIEW ANSWERS: YOUR EDUCATION

Why did you choose your university and what factors influenced your choice?

<u>Why this question is being asked</u>: To understand your decision making process and long term planning skills.

<u>Strategy</u>: Focus on what you thought you could gain for your career by attending the university that you did.

<u>Sample answer</u>: Well, I was happy to be accepted to my first choice, Hudson University. I had some friends who were a few years older than me that attended and they seemed to have a good experience. I was familiar with Hudson's strong business school and local contacts and that really sold me on the opportunity. I am really glad that I went and I still participate in alumni activities.

Discuss your educational background.

<u>Why this question is being asked</u>: To determine if your education meets or exceeds the requirements for the job.

<u>Strategy</u>: Provide an overview of your credentials but focus on your education that is most relevant to the job.

<u>Sample answer</u>: I have a bachelors and masters in finance from Hudson University. As an undergraduate, I minored in Art History. That minor has given me a better understanding

of the art business.

What's the most important thing you learned in school?

<u>Why this question is being asked</u>: To get a sense of what sort of information you value and how that has shaped you.

<u>Strategy</u>: Focus on a particular value, skill or area of knowledge that would be most applicable to the job.

<u>Sample answer</u>: The most important thing that I learned was how to prioritize my time. I finished my bachelors in three years instead of the usual four. I also interned and had a part-time job.

What training have you had for this job?

<u>Why this question is being asked</u>: To learn how ready you are for the job.

<u>Strategy</u>: Provide insight into both the formal and informal training that you have had.

<u>Sample answer</u>: I have several years of training in sales. In addition to being mentored and learning from seasoned professionals for five years in my last position, I worked in sales part time while I was in school and took several courses in sales and marketing.

Why did you choose your major?

<u>Why this question is being asked</u>: To gain a better understanding of you professional interests and goals at the time.

<u>Strategy</u>: Construct an answer that would be applicable for the job. If the major directly relates, it is an easier connection.

If the major is unrelated, focus on an aspect of the major or what you learned that is relevant to the position.

<u>Sample answer</u>: I chose communication because I felt that it is an essential tool, no matter what the field. My communication abilities have served me well in the sales field and I am glad that I chose it.

Why did you choose your degree subject?

<u>Why this question is being asked</u>: To gain a better understanding of you professional interests and goals at the time.

<u>Strategy</u>: Construct an answer that would be applicable for the job. If the major directly relates, it is an easier connection. If the major is unrelated, focus on an aspect of the major or what you learned that is relevant to the position.

<u>Sample answer</u>: I chose communication because I felt that it is an essential tool, no matter what the field. My communication abilities have served me well in the sales field and I am glad that I chose it.

What computer skills do you have?

<u>Why this question is being asked</u>: To understand if you have the computer skills necessary for the job.

<u>Strategy</u>: Concentrate on listing the computer skills that are most relevant to the position. Describe an example or two of how you used them successfully on the job.

<u>Sample answer</u>: I am proficient in Microsoft Word, Excel and PowerPoint. I've been asked by my boss to hold regular trainings in Excel so that other employees can learn some of the intricacies of the program.

What is a suggestion you've made at work that was implemented?

Why this question is being asked: To understand how your contributions are valued at work.

Strategy: Provide a relevant example that demonstrates that your contribution was valued, how it was implemented and ultimately, how it helped the company.

Sample answer: I suggested that instead of having all day meetings, that we have a one hour meeting bi-weekly in the mornings and break up the other meeting times into areas of specialization so that those who did not work in that area could concentrate on what they needed to do, so everyone maximized their time. The idea was well received and it helped employees to maximize their efficiency.

Tell me about your experiences at school.

Why this question is being asked: To understand how you maintain your professionalism in answering the question.

Strategy: Focus on the professional activities that you participated in, on and off campus, and what you gained. Avoid discussing any party or non-professional activities.

Sample answer: Being that Hudson University is based in the heart of the city, there were many professional activities that I participated in, on and off campus. I participated in the marketing club and started an entrepreneur club. I assisted one of my professors with his research in the field during my junior and senior years. Through the university, I was able to volunteer and help mentor children as well. So all in all, a busy but great 4 years!

What has been the most rewarding university experience?

<u>Why this question is being asked</u>: To learn about what experience you valued most and gain better insight into your priorities.

<u>Strategy</u>: Focus on an aspect of your experience that involved utilizing skills that would be important to a job, such as teamwork.

<u>Sample answer</u>: The most rewarding, and challenging, part of my experience was serving as the leader for the final class project. It required a lot of coordination in terms of schedules, getting everyone on the same page and working towards a plan. It was extremely rewarding when we reached the goal and received a group score of A.

On a scale of 1-10, how would you rate your vocabulary and grammar skills?

<u>Why this question is being asked</u>: The interviewer wants to get a better sense of your writing skills as well as your ability to be self critical.

<u>Strategy</u>: Provide a good but not perfect score. Highlight where you are strong but also where there is room for improvement.

<u>Sample answer</u>: I would say an eight. I believe that my vocabulary and grammar skills are quite strong, given my professional capabilities and background, but would certainly pale next to an accomplished editor or writing professor. I believe that there is always room for improvement. For example, 5 years ago, I considered myself to have strong grammar skills but when I look back on it now, I notice some mistakes.

How has your education prepared you for your job?

<u>Why this question is being asked</u>: To understand what educational qualifications you bring to the job.

<u>Strategy</u>: Focus on the subject matter that is relevant to the job as well as some of the soft skills you may have gained in an educational setting.

<u>Sample answer</u>: Well, of course working in the Accounting field, I feel that my accounting courses challenged me and prepared me well for the field. Equally important, I was prepared to be a better professional by being held accountable to meet deadlines as well as complete many tasks in a group setting.

What college subjects did you like best? Why?

<u>Why this question is being asked</u>: To gain a better understanding of your interests.

<u>Strategy</u>: Make a connection between the subject you enjoyed and the type of job you are interviewing for. The subject does not have to be directly related to the job as long as you make a connection.

<u>Sample answer</u>: My favorite subject was Speech. Before I took the class, I would not consider myself a confident speaker, especially speaking in front of a group! The class really challenged me and I gained a lot of confidence. I think back on that class often before I give a presentation to a large group.

What college subjects did you like least? Why?

<u>Why this question is being asked</u>: To get a better sense of what subject matters don't interest you.

<u>Strategy</u>: Provide a subject that is unrelated to the position.

<u>Sample answer</u>: Philosophy was my least favorite subject. Although the concept of abstract thought and debate is very interesting, I had a hard time wrapping myself up in it.

If you could do so, how would you plan your academic study differently?

<u>Why this question is being asked</u>: To see if you can learn from your mistakes.

<u>Strategy</u>: Focus on your pursuit of excellence as opposed to discussing any laziness or procrastination in school.

<u>Sample answer</u>: If anything, I would say that I came out of the starting gate too strong and things started to drag towards the end of the semester. I would have paced myself better and maintained my focus on term papers and finals.

What have you learned from participation in extracurricular activities?

<u>Why this question is being asked</u>: To learn how active you have been outside of required curriculum and what you learned from those situations.

<u>Strategy</u>: Focus on the skills that would be relevant and applicable for the job.

<u>Sample answer</u>: Being on the wrestling team allowed me to push myself harder than I ever had before physically. It taught me that you may set limits on yourself but if you work harder and don't give up that you can push through those self imposed limits to get to the next level.

Do you have plans for earning an advanced degree?

<u>Why this question is being asked</u>: To understand if you have a

plan to continue to learn new things and advance yourself.

Strategy: Even if you don't have a concrete plan at the moment, express an interest to continue your studies. It would be best if you can identify the type of degree or continued study that you plan to pursue.

Sample answer: Yes, I am in a masters degree program now in fact. I do believe that it is important to keep advancing my education in order to learn, keep growing and contribute more to my employer.

Did you face any particular problems when you transitioned from high school to college?

Why this question is being asked: To learn how well you transition to a new environment.

Strategy: Explain some of the challenges you encountered and what you did to adapt.

Sample answer: Going from high school to college was a major transition for me. My high school was very small and college was in another state and a very large institution. I had to learn the resources to properly manage: the way to register for classes, new study habits as well as learning how to use the school library properly. It was a challenge at first but I feel that I excelled.

How did you handle any differences you may have had with a professor?

Why this question is being asked: To learn how you may similarly manage a disagreement with a superior in the future, such as a supervisor.

Strategy: Provide a disagreement you may have had with a

professor, how you went about it and how it was ultimately resolved.

<u>Sample answer</u>: I was surprised to receive a C on a paper that I felt I should have received an A on. I asked to speak with the professor, not to argue my grade but learn where I might have gone wrong and how I could improve in the future. The professor felt the paper lacked originality and while well researched, did not further expand knowledge into the field. He gave me the opportunity to redo it and I received an A- on that paper and ultimately an A in the course.

Does your work relate to any studies you had in college?

<u>Why this question is being asked</u>: To understand how your education matches your work.

<u>Strategy</u>: Prove that you have a special expertise based on your strong academic foundation.

<u>Sample answer</u>: Certainly. I conduct extensive market research. My background in psychology has prepared me well in this field as I know how to prepare, conduct, and analyze the data gathered from surveys properly.

How important is GPA for obtaining a job in this field?

<u>Why this question is being asked</u>: To learn how you value education and its importance to success on the job.

<u>Strategy</u>: Provide a balanced answer that demonstrates the importance of grades but why other factors are more important as well.

<u>Sample answer</u>: I believe that demonstrating a strong GPA shows an understanding of the subject matter but there is much more to it than that. On the job, you have to always be willing to learn, put in the extra effort and be a team player in order to succeed. If someone can demonstrate those skills in an interview, that person should be given strong consideration for the job.

Do you have plans for continued study?

<u>Why this question is being asked</u>: To understand if you have a plan to continue to learn new things and advance yourself.

<u>Strategy</u>: Even if you don't have a concrete plan at the moment, express an interest to continue your studies. It would be best if you can identify the type of degree or continued study that you plan to pursue.

<u>Sample answer</u>: Yes, I am currently enrolled in a master's program. I do believe that it is important to keep advancing my education in order to learn, keep growing and contribute more to my employer.

What were your favorite classes in school?

<u>Why this question is being asked</u>: To learn what areas of school interested you.

<u>Strategy</u>: Two strategies would work here. Choose the one that you feel would give new information to the interviewer. Either focus on you qualifications by speaking about courses which are relevant to the job, or show your well roundedness by demonstrating an interest in an unrelated area.

<u>Sample answer</u>: Being a banker, I did enjoy the finance classes but I also enjoyed taking art history. It allowed me to learn about a field that I was previously unfamiliar with and gave me something interesting to talk about when I meet new people.

What courses did you enjoy most in college?

<u>Why this question is being asked</u>: To gain a better understanding of your interests.

<u>Strategy</u>: Make a connection between the subjects you enjoyed and the type of job you are interviewing for. The subject does not have to be directly related to the job as long as you make a connection.

<u>Sample answer</u>: I enjoyed the balance between liberal arts and business classes. I felt that it was important to balance my studies beyond just a vocational pursuit. The ability to study art history in the morning and finance in the afternoon helped me to become a well rounded person.

Tell me about your education.

<u>Why this question is being asked</u>: To understand how you maintain your professionalism in answering the question.

<u>Strategy</u>: Focus on the professional activities that you participated in, on and off campus, and what you gained. Avoid discussing any party of non-professional activities.

Sample answer: Being that Hudson University is based in the heart of the city, there were many professional activities that I participated in, on and off campus. I participated in the marketing club and started an entrepreneur club. I assisted one of my professors with his research in the field during my junior and senior years. Through the university, I was able to volunteer and help mentor children as well. So all in all, a busy but great 4 years!

What were your favorite activities at school?

Why this question is being asked: To understand what you participated in at school outside of a classroom setting and why you enjoyed those activities.

Strategy: Focus on the skills or experience gained from activities that have some relation to the job you are pursuing.

Sample answer: My school had many chances to participate in social justice activities and I enjoyed partaking in that whenever I could. I helped to organize fund raisers, schedule trips to visit the elderly and mentor teenagers. It allowed me to gain confidence in my leadership abilities and become a better planner.

Describe a time when you had to make a difficult choice between your professional and academic life.

Why this question is being asked: To learn about your priorities and how you make difficult choices.

Strategy: Provide an example of when you had to make a choice. Describe why a choice was necessary and the end result.

Sample answer: Over the summer of my freshman year, I

volunteered in a nursing home helping the activities director. The director retired and I was offered the position. I enjoyed the work and was interested, but my goal was to focus on school so I had to turn it down.

In what ways have your college experiences prepared you for a career?

<u>Why this question is being asked</u>: To understand what you gained from your college experience that would be applicable on the job.

<u>Strategy</u>: Provide concrete examples of how your coursework and other activities helped to prepare you.

<u>Sample answer</u>: My college's requirement to take two additional economic classes allowed me to gain an understanding of world markets, which has made me a more informed business person. Group work was an essential element of most classes and I became a better team player as well as a leader. My heavy course load allowed me to better prioritize my time which has been extremely valuable on the job.

How do you think you have changed personally since you started university?

<u>Why this question is being asked</u>: To understand how you've grown as a professional since you started school.

<u>Strategy</u>: Use examples of changes that would be applicable to the job.

<u>Sample answer</u>: I became more confident in my abilities. I've been put in the position to become a leader and prove myself. I am better at managing my time. I can communicate more

effectively.

Describe your most rewarding college experience.

<u>Why this question is being asked</u>: To understand what you participated in at school outside of a classroom setting and why you enjoyed those activities.

<u>Strategy</u>: Focus on the skills or experience gained from an experience that has some relation to the job you are pursuing.

<u>Sample answer</u>: My school provided many chances to participate in social justice activities and I enjoyed partaking in that whenever I could. I helped to organize a fund raiser for the homeless. I was named the team captain and was responsible for recruiting participants and overseeing the work of others in maintaining the budget, booking the venue, creating the itinerary and promoting the event. It was extremely challenging and stressful as well but very rewarding. We ended up raising $22,000.

Did you enjoy college?

<u>Why this question is being asked</u>: To understand what type of experience is a good fit, or a poor fit, for you and why.

<u>Strategy</u>: Focus on the aspects that you enjoyed and why as well as reflect back on how you could have gained more from the experience.

<u>Sample answer</u>: Well, I did but I was in a rush to enter the working world so I didn't enjoy it as much as I should have. I participated in many extracurricular activities and took a heavy course load but things seemed to pass by quickly. If I could do it over, I'd try to maintain my perspective that this is a once in a lifetime experience and enjoy it a bit more.

Why do you think graduates in [your degree subject] would be good [job role you have applied for]?

<u>Why this question is being asked</u>: To understand if your degree is relevant to the job.

<u>Strategy</u>: If you degree is not directly applicable to the job, make a connection as to why it is relevant. Give an example to prove your point.

<u>Sample answer</u>: My degree is in psychology. I believe that it is directly applicable to business as it allows me to understand people better, analyze information and think critically. My research abilities that were well developed in my psychology classes in college have come in handy on the job as we build profiles of our consumer base.

Knowing what you know now about your college experience, would you make the same decisions?

<u>Why this question is being asked</u>: To learn about your ability to reflect on a situation and learn from it.

<u>Strategy</u>: Portray yourself as someone that does not dwell on the past but someone who can learn from certain situations and improve them.

<u>Sample answer</u>: In hindsight, there are always things that we could have done differently and I would have knowing what I now know. I would have picked better study partners, balanced my course load a bit better and modified my study techniques. These are all things that I learned through experience. There was no way to know many of these in advance so I learned from them and moved on.

What contributions have you made to a group project?

<u>Why this question is being asked</u>: To understand what type of team player you are.

<u>Strategy</u>: Provide relevant examples that show you are not only a team player but can take on leadership roles as well.

<u>Sample answer</u>: I have participated in many group projects. My exact role varied based on the expertise of the other group members. In certain situations, the group felt it would be best if I took on a leadership and coordination role and in other situations I specialized, such as concentrating on a certain area of research or putting together the final presentation. No matter the role, I was always happy to contribute.

Do you have education relevant to this position?

<u>Why this question is being asked:</u> To learn what relevant skills and education you have that would be of value to the employer.

<u>Strategy</u>: List your most relevant skills. Provide an example or two to demonstrate your expertise.

<u>Sample answer</u>: Yes. I studied psychology as an undergraduate, which allowed me to become a better researcher, writer and communicator- all valuable skills in the business field. I completed a certificate program in Finance and Accounting at Hudson University. This certificate allowed me to get the crucial business underpinnings that I believe are necessary for this position. I have a variety of skills that would be useful in this role including my bilingual communication ability and excellent grasp of database

systems. In my last position, I was called upon to troubleshoot any issues with the database and resolve them while working with the information technology team.

Is graduate school important?

<u>Why this question is being asked</u>: To learn how much you value education and if you understand the education requirements for the field.

<u>Strategy</u>: If graduate school is an important element of excelling in the industry, emphasize why you feel it is important.

<u>Sample answer</u>: Yes, I do feel that graduate school is important. From speaking to many senior executives in this industry, it was recommended that I obtain an MBA after gaining 5-7 years experience in the field. I do plan to do that one day.

Are you currently taking or enrolled to take any job related educational courses?

<u>Why this question is being asked</u>: To understand how you are advancing yourself.

<u>Strategy</u>: Discuss any coursework that you are pursuing, whether it is of a formal or informal nature.

<u>Sample answer</u>: I have been accepted for a master's program in September. I will be going to class one late night a week and on Saturdays. I regularly advance my knowledge by participating in online tutorials.

If you could improve anything about your college, what would it be?

<u>Why this question is being asked</u>: To understand how you analyze a situation and make suggestions into how it could be improved.

<u>Strategy</u>: If possible, focus on an area of improvement at your school that would relate to the job.

<u>Sample answer</u>: There were so many great professional opportunities in college but a lot of it was lost due to ill timed planning and poor customer service on the administration's part. Sometimes, when you went into a college office for help, you felt like you did something wrong by just asking a question. It served as an important reminder to me when I entered the working world to treat everyone with the utmost respect and do anything I can to help.

How will the academic program and coursework you've taken benefit your career?

<u>Why this question is being asked</u>: To understand if your education is relevant to the job.

<u>Strategy</u>: If your degree is not directly applicable to the job, make a connection as to why it is relevant. Give an example to prove your point.

<u>Sample answer</u>: My degree is in psychology. I believe that it is applicable to business as it allows me to understand people better, analyze information and think critically. The strong research abilities that I developed in my psychology classes have come in handy many times on the job as we build profiles of our consumer base.

Are you the type of student for whom conducting independent research has been a positive experience?

<u>Why this question is being asked</u>: To learn if you are good at conducting research and if you can work independently.

<u>Strategy</u>: Demonstrate that you are the type of person who can work independently and conduct top notch research.

<u>Sample answer</u>: Yes, I did enjoy conducting independent research. After receiving instruction from my mentor, I was able to conduct extensive research into the sports marketing industry. The work was accepted into a scholarly journal and I got to present it at a conference.

Describe the type of teacher who had the most beneficial influence upon you.

<u>Why this question is being asked</u>: To learn what type of mentor you relate to most and why.
<u>Strategy</u>: Focus on an experience with a teacher that provided a beneficial lesson.

<u>Sample answer</u>: Mr. Smith was my high school chemistry teacher. Even as a kid, I could tell which teachers were looking at the clock for the day to end and which ones were passionate about helping students. Mr. Smith really went the extra mile to see his students succeed. I try to take the same type of passion to what I do and give it my all.

Describe the type of teacher that has created the most beneficial learning experience for you.

<u>Why this question is being asked</u>: To learn what type of mentor you relate to best and why.

<u>Strategy</u>: Focus on an experience with a teacher that provided a beneficial lesson.

Sample answer: Ms. Smith was my high school chemistry teacher. She was great at explaining the subject matter but her dedication had a bigger influence on me. Even as a kid, I could tell which teacher was looking at the clock and which ones were passionate about helping students. Mr. Smith really went the extra mile to see her students succeed. I try to take the same type of passion to what I do and give it my all.

Do you think that your grades are indication of your academic achievement?

Why this question is being asked: To understand if you reached your full potential and if not, why.

Strategy: If you did not receive straight A's, explain how you could have improved and why you didn't meet your potential.

Sample answer: I do believe that I had the ability to get an A in each class and since I did not, my GPA does not reflect my full capabilities. There were some missteps I made along the way, such as concentrating on the wrong areas before the test. I learned from my mistakes and improved and I think that the grades in my junior and senior years more fully reflect my capabilities.

How was your transition from high school to college?

Why this question is being asked: To learn how well you transition to a new environment.

Strategy: Explain some of the challenges you encountered and what you did to adapt.

Sample answer: Going from high school to college was a major transition for me. My high school was very small and my college was in another state and a very large institution. I had to learn the resources to properly manage: the way to register for classes, new study habits and learning how to use the school library properly. It was a challenge at first but I excelled in the end.

How have you differed from your professors in evaluating your performance?

<u>Why this question is being asked</u>: To learn how you can manage a disagreement with a superior.

<u>Strategy</u>: Provide a disagreement you may have had with a professor, how you went about it and how it was ultimately resolved.

<u>Sample answer</u>: I was surprised to receive a C on a paper of the quality that I felt I normally would have received an A on in another class. I asked to speak with the professor, not to argue my grade but learn where I might have gone wrong and how I could improve in the future. The professor felt the paper lacked originality and while well researched, did not further expand knowledge into the field. He gave me the opportunity to redo it and I received an A- on that paper and ultimately an A in the course.

How has college changed you as a person?

<u>Why this question is being asked</u>: To learn how you grow in a new situation.

<u>Strategy</u>: Focus on how you've become a better professional.

<u>Sample answer</u>: College was an excellent transition point to become a professional. I learned more about responsibility, teamwork and accountability that has served me well on the job.

Give an example of something you've done in school that demonstrates your willingness to work hard.

<u>Why this question is being asked</u>: To gain more insight into your work ethic.

<u>Strategy</u>: Provide a relevant example that demonstrates your work ethic. Explain why you chose to take on this challenge, why it was difficult and what you ultimately accomplished.

<u>Sample answer</u>: I was interested in gaining more on the job experience than just a summer internship. While a fulltime student, I chose to take on an internship in the city for 25 hours per week. It was challenging to balance my schoolwork and the internship with the rest of life's demands but it was worth it. I grew my understanding of the business world and more importantly, became more proficient in prioritizing my time.

Describe the last time that you undertook a project that demanded a lot of initiative.

<u>Why this question is being asked:</u> To understand if you are good and taking on a challenge and showing initiative.
<u>Strategy</u>: Explain a challenge that you took on that would be relevant to the job you are interviewing for. Explain why you took on the project, what steps you took to complete it and what the end result was.

<u>Sample answer</u>: My company had been using several databases to enter the same information. I wanted to streamline the process so I decided to work with the IT team to create one database that covered all of the necessary information. It was a long process, with several setbacks, but I saw it through and ended up saving the company from lots of wasted time.

Does your work relate to any experiences you had in college?

<u>Why this question is being asked</u>: To understand how your education matches your work.

<u>Strategy</u>: Prove that you have a special expertise or knowledge in what you do based on your strong academic foundation.

<u>Sample answer</u>: Certainly. I conduct extensive market research. My background in psychology has prepared me well in this field as I know how to conduct valid surveys and analyze the data properly.

What courses have proved to be the most valuable to you in your work?

<u>Why this question is being asked</u>: To understand if your degree is relevant to the job.

<u>Strategy</u>: If your degree is not directly applicable to the job, make a connection as to why it is relevant. Give an example to prove your point.

<u>Sample answer</u>: The courses I took in Psychology. I believe that it is directly applicable to business as it allows me to understand people better, analyze information and think critically. My research abilities that were well developed in my Psychology classes in college have come in handy many times on the job as we build profiles of our consumer base.

What courses do you wish you had taken that would have better prepared you?

<u>Why this question is being asked</u>: To understand what you may regret or what you've learned in hindsight that may be important.

<u>Strategy</u>: Focus on an area that may have been helpful to have learned but is not a major gap in your knowledge base.

<u>Sample answer</u>: Well in hindsight, it would have been nice to have taken a marketing class or two as I would have started out with a stronger foundation in the field. Thankfully, I was able to gain an excellent understanding of the basics during my first 3 years on the job.

If you were a college student again, what would you do differently to prepare for this job?

<u>Why this question is being asked</u>: To understand what you've learned in hindsight that may be important.

<u>Strategy</u>: Provide an example of how you would have prepared more for this niche field.

<u>Sample answer</u>: I do feel very prepared given my experience in the field and general education in the field of Marketing. If I would have known that my industry of focus would become international markets, I would have taken additional coursework in international business and advanced Spanish courses.

How important are grades for obtaining a job in this field?

<u>Why this question is being asked</u>: To learn how you value education and its importance to success on the job.

<u>Strategy</u>: Provide a balanced answer that demonstrates the importance of grades but why other factors are more important as well.

<u>Sample answer</u>: I believe that demonstrating good grades shows an understanding of the subject matter but there is much more to it than that. On the job, you have to always be

willing to learn, put in the extra effort and be a team player in order to succeed. If someone can demonstrate those skills in an interview, he/she should be given strong consideration for the job as well.

What is the best educational preparation for this career?

<u>Why this question is being asked</u>: To learn what you feel would be the best way to be prepared to enter the field.

<u>Strategy</u>: Emphasize what preparation you already have as the essential preparedness for the field, whether it be formal education, informal learning or on the job experience.

<u>Sample answer</u>: I feel that there is no better preparation than learning on the job. This is why I completed 3 internships in the field to learn more about the culture and expectations of the field as well as to prove myself.

How do you think [name of your school]'s reputation is viewed when it comes to hiring?

<u>Why this question is being asked</u>: To learn how much you think the reputation of a school will help you to get a job versus having to prove yourself.

<u>Strategy</u>: Explain that while you the think that the name of a school has value for getting noticed, that the individual is the one that will be responsible for getting the job.

<u>Sample answer</u>: Well, Hudson University does have a great reputation and having that name on my resume was probably helpful for getting the interview but it is up to the person to prove themselves. I believe that you really have to hire based on the candidate and not on the school.

If you were entering this career today, would you change your

preparation in any way to better facilitate entry?

<u>Why this question is being asked</u>: To understand what you've learned in hindsight that may be important.

<u>Strategy</u>: Make it clear that you are well prepared for the field given your education and experience but provide an example of how you would have prepared more for this niche field.

<u>Sample answer</u>: I do feel very prepared given my experience in the field and general education in the field of marketing. If I would have known that my career focus would be on international markets, I would have taken additional coursework in international business and advanced Spanish courses.

Do you apply the skills and knowledge learned at school in your work?

<u>Why this question is being asked</u>: To understand what additional skills you have that would be valuable in the workplace.

<u>Strategy</u>: Focus on the relevant knowledge and skills you learned in the classroom.

<u>Sample answer</u>: Yes, I was given a very solid foundation of understanding accounting principles that I utilize regularly as part of my job. Additionally, I learned some of the soft skills necessary to succeed in a work environment such as teamwork and communication skills.

What do you like best about your school?

<u>Why this question is being asked</u>: To learn more about what interests you and how it may relate to the job.

<u>Strategy</u>: Focus on something that would be of value or interest to the interviewer.

<u>Sample answer</u>: My school offered many chances to participate in social justice activities and I enjoyed partaking in them whenever I could. I helped to organize fund raisers, schedule trips to visit the elderly and mentor teenagers. It allowed me to gain confidence in my leadership abilities and become a better planner.

Please describe your own roles and functions in school, clubs, or other groups.

<u>Why this question is being asked</u>: To learn how active you have been in participating in roles that are extracurricular or outside of your own responsibilities.

<u>Strategy</u>: Focus on activities that would be relevant to the interviewer. Demonstrate your ability to take on additional responsibilities, assume leadership roles and manage your time well.

<u>Sample answer</u>: My school offered many chances to participate in social justice activities and I enjoyed partaking in them whenever I could. I helped to organize fund raisers, schedule trips to visit the elderly and mentor teenagers. It allowed me to gain confidence in my leadership abilities and become a better planner.

Do you feel that your grades are a good indicator of your ability?

<u>Why this question is being asked</u>: To understand if you reached your full potential and if not, why.

<u>Strategy</u>: If you did not receive straight A's, explain how you could have improved and why you didn't meet your potential.

<u>Sample answer</u>: I do believe that I had the ability to get an A in each class and since I did not, my GPA does not reflect my full capabilities. There were some missteps I made along the way, such as concentrating on the wrong areas before the test. I learned from my mistakes and improved. I think that the grades in my junior and senior years more fully reflect my capabilities.

What would cause you to miss an assignment or be tardy?

<u>Why this question is being asked</u>: To understand your ability and motivation to meet deadlines and what might prevent you from that.

<u>Strategy</u>: Make it clear that you have an excellent track record of making deadlines and it would have to be something out of the ordinary to miss one.

<u>Sample answer</u>: Perhaps a hurricane, tornado, storm or other unforeseen act of nature? Actually, even then I am unlikely to miss the deadline. Once I have a deadline to work towards, I do everything I can to provide top notch work and complete the assignment well before the deadline.

Tell me about your undergraduate university experience.

<u>Why this question is being asked</u>: To understand what you felt was memorable and important to share during the interview.

<u>Strategy</u>: Focus on experiences such as your coursework and extracurricular activities that would be important to the job.

<u>Sample answer</u>: I majored in psychology. It allowed me to learn more about how people make decisions and deal with things. I improved my writing, communication and teamwork abilities. I was a member of the fencing team. I also participated in several extracurricular activities, including the Business Club and Social Action Committee.

If you were hiring a graduate for this position, what qualities would you look for?

<u>Why this question is being asked</u>: To gain a better understanding about what you know about the position as well as what you feel would be the essential skills and qualities for the job.

<u>Strategy</u>: Demonstrate your knowledge of the position requirements and emphasize some of your own strengths as being important for the position.

<u>Sample answer</u>: Well, I know that you would need someone with an excellent understanding of accounting principles in a non-profit environment. In addition to the knowledge gained in the classroom, it would be helpful to have some on-the-job and internship experience in the field. I would also want someone who is a team player, dependable and has a "can-do" attitude.

6 WINNING INTERVIEW ANSWERS: YOUR PERSONALITY & MOTIVATION

What do you know about our company?

<u>Why this question is being asked</u>: To learn if you have done your research into the company because you are especially interested in this position, or if you are just applying for any old job.

<u>Strategy</u>: You don't have to give the company history dating back to 1925, but show an understanding of the core business, how the company operates and if possible, what you know about the specific department you are interviewing for.

<u>Sample answer</u>: I have been following your company closely for the last several years. Your company became an innovator in the industry by adapting the use of cutting edge fulfillment technologies. You are data driven and each employee is empowered to succeed or fail on his or her own. The research department has been lauded for its use of several mathematical principles to deliver results.

What interests you about this job opening?

<u>Why this question is being asked</u>: To know the reason you applied for this particular job. The interviewer wants to know if you are especially interested in this position, or are

just looking for any job without a specific draw to this company.

<u>Strategy</u>: Provide specific reasons as to why this job interests you at this time and is an excellent fit.

<u>Sample answer</u>: My experience in research has built to this point. Given the cutting edge techniques used by your company and your place as an industry leader, I know that by working here I can contribute and grow to become a mutual partner in success with your company.

What salary range are you looking for?

<u>Why this question is being asked</u>: To determine your expectations of salary as compared to what the company would like to pay.

<u>Strategy</u>: Based on your prior research, provide a salary range and not just one number. Make it clear that it is not only about the salary.

<u>Sample answer</u>: Well, it is not only about the salary to me as I am looking to contribute and become a partner in success with your organization. I am seeking a salary within the range of $90,000-115,000 per year, depending on the benefits and incentives of course.

What were your expectations for your previous job and to what extent were they met?

<u>Why this question is being asked</u>: To understand what occurred in your last work experience and why it was a positive or a negative experience.

<u>Strategy</u>: Focus on the positives of why that job was the right fit at that time and why now is the right time to move on.

Sample answer: My expectations were to be in a progressively responsible position and to contribute within a role requiring mid-career experience. It was a wonderful opportunity to contribute for the past five years and now I am looking to utilize that experience and move to the next great opportunity.

What can you do for this company?

Why this question is being asked: To learn what your expectations are in contributing to the company.

Strategy: Demonstrate your knowledge of the needs of the company and the responsibilities of the position by giving a specific answer.

Sample answer: As the operations manager, I would like to contribute to a more effective flow of processes and cost reduction for the company by implementing measures to improve shipping times and reduce the occurrence of goods becoming damaged in delivery. I would take some of the best practices that I learned over my career and partner with company management to learn the methods that work best here.

What do you find are the most difficult decisions to make?

Why this question is being asked: To learn about your decision making process.

Strategy: Consider the decisions that you would have to make in the role and use one as an example. Provide a reason why the decision might be difficult and how you would approach it.

Sample answer: The most difficult decisions are the ones that affect the lives of people. Most decisions that an executive would make have a major impact on the lives of workers. I give much weight to this fact when considering the best course of action.

Why should we hire you?

<u>Why this question is being asked</u>:   To give you the opportunity to effectively sell yourself for the job and convince the company to want to hire you.

<u>Strategy</u>: Confidently reinforce your strongest qualities, experience and abilities for this job to demonstrate why you are the right fit for the job.

<u>Sample answer</u>: I understand this industry as I've worked my way up to this role by successfully holding progressively responsible positions for the last 15 years. I have an excellent understanding of your company culture and needs and can work effectively in a team to solve your greatest challenges. I am a tireless worker who will do whatever is necessary to get the job done right, before the deadline and with minimal error.

What is more important to you: money or work?

<u>Why this question is being asked</u>:   To learn about your value system and what you prioritize as a professional.

<u>Strategy</u>: Focus on the work as to make it clear that the more successful you are at work, the more likely you are to earn greater monetary reward.

<u>Sample answer</u>: The work is more important to me because I know that when I prove myself as a significant contributor to the company that the money will follow. An employee and

the employer can only be successful if they consider each other partners in success.

Where else have you applied?

<u>Why this question is being asked</u>: To understand what other opportunities you are considering and who the company may have to compete with to get your services.

<u>Strategy</u>: Make it clear to the company that you are active in the market and considering other opportunities but that you are very interested in this one.

<u>Sample answer</u>: As it is a good time to explore where I may fit best in the market, I have been interviewing with several companies in this industry as well as some related fields to determine where I would fit best. My interest in this company is very genuine and I would like to continue exploring further.

Are you willing to relocate?

<u>Why this </u>question is being asked: If you are out of the area, the company wants to know if you are serious about the job and would relocate.

<u>Strategy</u>: Make it clear that your interest is genuine in the position and you have begun the exploratory stages to learn more about the area.

<u>Sample answer</u>: Oh yes, I am very serious about considering this area for my next move. Along with flying in for the interview on Thursday, I've taken Friday off in order to get a better sense of the neighborhood, check out schools for my kids and learn more about the community.

How do you handle pressure?

<u>Why this question is being asked</u>: As work is naturally stressful, the interviewer wants to know how you manage yours.

<u>Strategy</u>: Be honest that you do get stressed. Provide concrete examples to show how you can manage the stress.

<u>Sample answer</u>: I try to remain calm and prioritize my time when thinking about what needs to be done first. If it is an especially stressful time of year, I make sure to spend my lunch away from my desk and to get some exercise. I find that it makes me feel refreshed so that I have the energy to deal with the work.

What questions do you have for me?

<u>Why this question is being asked</u>: To provide you with the opportunity to gain additional insight into the job.

<u>Strategy</u>: This is not the time to think, "Now, it's my turn!" and ask questions about the salary or work hours. Focus on questions that show you have a strong understanding of the industry and needs of the position and to gain greater insight into what the company truly values in a worker.

<u>Sample answer</u>: Given the transition of databases from onsite servers to cloud based, how do you feel the industry will change?

What are the biggest challenges facing someone in this role?

What would you like the person in this role to have achieved after 6 months?

Aren't you overqualified for this position?

<u>Why this question is being asked</u>: To determine why you are

applying for a job that you appear to be overqualified for.

<u>Strategy</u>: Explain why your skills and qualifications are a good fit for this job and why you have a serious interest even though it appears to be more of a junior level position.

<u>Sample answer</u>: I think that I am a good fit for the job, neither under nor overqualified. Although my last title was "Manager", it was with a smaller company than this one.

Would you lie for the company?

<u>Why this question is being asked</u>: To get a sense of your moral compass.

<u>Strategy</u>: Make it clear that you would not lie.

<u>Sample answer</u>: No, I could not lie for the company.

What can you tell us about our company?

<u>Why this question is being asked</u>: To learn if your interest in the company is specific and if you have done your research, or if you are just applying to hundreds of companies looking for any old job.

<u>Strategy</u>: You don't have to give the company history dating back to 1925, but show an understanding of the core business, how the company operates and if possible, what you know about the specific department you are interviewing for.

<u>Sample answer</u>: Given your position as a leader in the industry, I have been following your company closely for the last several years. Your company became an innovator in the industry by adapting the use of cutting edge fulfillment technologies. You are data driven and each employee is

empowered to succeed or fail on his or her own. The research department has been lauded for its use of several mathematical principles to deliver results.

What do you know about our competitors?

<u>Why this question is being asked</u>: To know if you understand the market and have done sufficient research.

<u>Strategy</u>: Prove that you understand the industry in which this company exists.

<u>Sample answer</u>: You are a major player in the world of social networking, and there are several major players in the industry as well. Facebook is the number one social networking platform while LinkedIn is for business networking. Twitter is for having short conversations…

How did you hear about this position?

<u>Why this question is being asked</u>: To learn if you have a passive or active interest in the job and possibly, if someone referred you.

<u>Strategy</u>: Wherever possible, it is important to demonstrate an active interest in the position.

<u>Sample answer</u>: As I have been interested in pursuing a job here for a while, I regularly check the company website. When I found a position listed in which I would be a strong candidate, I reached out to Bob Smith in your marketing department, as we are long time colleagues. He suggested that I apply.

Would you work weekends?

<u>Why this question is being asked</u>: To get a sense of your

schedule availability and commitment to the company.

<u>Strategy</u>: If it is the type of job where most of the business is on the weekends, such as retail or food services, the answer would have to be yes. If it is a job with traditional hours, make it clear that you would in special circumstances.

<u>Sample answer</u>: I would be ready to pitch in when needed. As weekends are usually family time for me, I would like to stay on top of my work when things are busy by coming in early, working through lunch and staying late. I know during the busy season that it may not be enough time so I would come in when I am needed.

How would you deal with an angry customer?

<u>Why this question is being asked</u>: To understand your process for best managing an interaction with an angry customer.

<u>Strategy</u>: Explain how you maintain your professionalism while dealing with a difficult situation.

<u>Sample answer</u>: If the person is already irate, the most important thing to do is to remain calm. Instead of concentrating on the volume of the person speaking, I would listen to what the actual problem is. I would consider how I can best deal with it or if I could not, how to best facilitate a connection to the person that could. I think people just want to be listened to and treated with respect. Once it is clear that you are doing both of those things, managing the actual problem becomes much easier.

How would you fire someone?

<u>Why this question is being asked</u>: If you are put in the position of manager, this is a likely occurrence at some point. <u>Strategy</u>: Explain how you would follow company protocols and try to make it as comfortable a situation as possible. <u>Sample answer</u>: I would check with human resources as to company best practices for managing the situation. I would like to provide the person plenty of time to ask questions and know that he/she is being heard, even if it did not work out in this job. I would explain the things that the person had done right on the job and what things were done poorly and why it would not work out here.

Why do you want this job?

<u>Why this question is being asked</u>: To understand why you want this job, not just any job.

<u>Strategy</u>: Provide clarity as to your serious interest in the job and why this role and company is the right fit for you.

<u>Sample answer</u>: I have worked my whole career for an opportunity like this. I would have the opportunity to apply my industry experience and team building expertise in this role. The organizational culture of teamwork fits my work style perfectly. Given the company size and projected growth, I know that this would be a great place for me to grow as well.

What is the most difficult thing about working with you?

<u>Why this question is being asked</u>: To understand how you work with others.

<u>Strategy</u>: Focus on something that others might find challenging but is really a strength that you would bring to the company.

Sample answer: I give 100% and I expect the same from others. I am very driven to succeed and I always give my all in providing the best work and getting things done well before the deadline.

Are you willing to make sacrifices for this company?

Why this question is being asked: To get a sense of your dedication to the company.

Strategy: Make it clear that you would and provide a relevant example.

Sample answer: Of course. When a company puts trust in me, I have to live up to that. If there is a major project or deadline coming up, I'll be sacrificing personal and family time in order to get the job done.

Do you know anyone who works with our company?

Why this question is being asked: To determine if there is someone within the company who can vouch for you.

Strategy: Be aware of whom you know that works for the company before you go on the interview. Even if you don't think you know anyone there, check LinkedIn as you might be surprised.

Sample answer: I do. Bob Smith, who works in the accounting department, was a colleague of mine at Flexco. We don't have a chance to catch up often, but I know he has been here for awhile and really enjoys the culture.

What will you do if you don't get this position?

Why this question is being asked: To learn how you deal with rejection.

<u>Strategy</u>: Explain how you would take steps to improve yourself in order to put yourself in a better position next time.

<u>Sample answer</u>: I would do my best to learn from the situation in order to improve. I would consider how I presented myself and if I made it clear how my skills and experience best matched the position and why I thought I was a great fit. I would consider what I was lacking that another candidate may have brought to the table in order to improve. I'd want to be ready the next time a similar opportunity presented itself.

How do you take direction?

<u>Why this question is being asked</u>: To understand how you would respond to management directives to meet company goals.

<u>Strategy</u>: Make it clear that you are someone who can follow directions well, but that you are not afraid to ask for clarity and provide input as well.

<u>Sample answer</u>: I am good at following directions. I understand that my supervisor has the responsibility of making sure the company meets its goals by organizing the workload amongst employees, and the insight to do so effectively. I am not afraid to ask questions if I need more clarity though, and if the timing seems right and my supervisor seems open to it, provide some suggestions as well.

Do you prefer working with others or alone?

<u>Why this question is being asked</u>: To determine what type of

job you like best: working solo or in a team.

Strategy: Most positions require a fair amount of work in both capacities, so hedge your bets, and make it clear that you can work both ways.

Sample answer: I really enjoy working with co-workers as we can rely upon one another and work together to meet our goals. But I also don't mind working alone as it allows me to be solely responsible for the assignment. My current job is a healthy mix of the two.

Can you summarize the contribution you would make to our organization?

Why this question is being asked: To determine if you understand the position and the goals that the company would want met.

Strategy: Think back to what you've learned about the position and emphasize the goals that you would meet.

Sample answer: In the role of call center manager, I would train reps. to effectively deal with customers and increase customer satisfaction. I would decrease time that customers spend on the phone by 25% and increase the satisfaction rate by a third. I would move us to a technology based model and allow us to cut down on the number of reps. that we require.

In what kind of work environment are you most comfortable?

<u>Why this question is being asked</u>: To determine if you are a proper fit for the company culture.

<u>Strategy</u>: Consider what you've learned about the work environment of the position you are interviewing for and emphasize some of those attributes.

<u>Sample answer</u>: I am most comfortable working in a team based environment where we can work collaboratively to meet goals. I like an environment where everyone has an open door policy and you can feel free to ask questions. I work best in an office where no one is watching the clock until they can get home because they are excited to be there and continue to contribute.

Why do you want to work for us and not for our competitor?

<u>Why this question is being asked</u>: To understand why this company is the ideal fit for you.

<u>Strategy</u>: Consider what qualities make this company unique in the industry as compared to the competition.

<u>Sample answer</u>: Well, I really respect that this company is a family business. I've found that corporations only care about the quarterly reports and it is easy to lose sight of the most important bottom line for business: the customers.

If offered this position, how long would you plan on staying with our company?

<u>Why this question is being asked</u>: To determine how long you are willing to stay and if the company should risk investing in you.

<u>Strategy</u>: Provide clarity as to why this is the type of opportunity that you would be interested in for the long term.

<u>Sample answer</u>: I feel that this is the type of company in which I could set down roots. I plan to stay here as long as I am challenged and can contribute on a high level. I love this field and this is where I want to be. Everything that I've learned informally and formally about your company makes me feel that I'd be here for the long term, if given the opportunity.

What would you do differently if you were in charge of this company?

<u>Why this question is being asked</u>: To understand what you think about the company now and if you have considered ways for the company to improve.

<u>Strategy</u>: Be cautious here in saying anything overly negative about the company but you do want to provide an answer that shows you've considered ways that the company could improve.

<u>Sample answer</u>: As your history of success shows, you are doing so many things right and I would like to get the experience of learning about the company before I suggest any major improvements. I would say that while your presence in traditional bookstores is strong, there could be some improvement in ebook marketing as the numbers do

show that ebooks are outselling traditional books in many cases.

Do you consider yourself a leader?

<u>Why this question is being asked</u>: To determine if you see leadership qualities in yourself.

<u>Strategy</u>: Make it clear that you do consider yourself a leader and provide a relevant example that proves it.

<u>Sample answer</u>: I do consider myself a leader. I am always ready to share my expertise and provide counsel to those who are learning. When there is a new project or initiative underway, I have volunteered to take the lead and steer the project.

What criteria do you use for evaluating success?

<u>Why this question is being asked</u>: To understand how you determine success for yourself and others.

<u>Strategy</u>: Explain the steps you take to evaluate if something was successful, with the priority of meeting company objectives.

<u>Sample answer</u>: To evaluate success, I first have to consider whether we met the company objectives. Did we hit the sales targets while staying within budget? Beyond hitting the targets, I would examine if we used our time and resources as efficiently as possible.

Walk me through the important points on your resume.

<u>Why this question is being asked</u>: As the interviewer may not have had the opportunity to review your resume extensively before the interview, he/she would like to hear about the most important parts of your background.

<u>Strategy</u>: Don't tell your whole work or professional history but discuss the most salient points of your background.

<u>Sample answer</u>: I've been in my last position since 2003. I lead a team of 20 sales agents. I have increased sales by 5-7% every year while cutting costs by 8-10% each year. I studied psychology in school and worked my way up from a sales coordinator in a niche firm to a management position in a Fortune 50 company. I am skilled in several database programs and Microsoft applications. I recently completed my masters in communications at Hudson University.

How do you stay up-to-date in this industry?

<u>Why this question is being asked</u>: To determine if you maintain a pulse of trends in the industry.

<u>Strategy</u>: Provide multiple resources that you utilize to stay up to date.

<u>Sample answer</u>: I feel that it is important to utilize multiple resources to stay up to date. Every day, I check the industry business websites. I subscribe to the industry newsletter. I attended two or three conferences every year. I participate in discussion forums on LinkedIn. I also schedule two or three networking meetings with industry professionals every month to hear what is happening on the ground.

What is your definition of intelligence?

<u>Why this question is being asked</u>: Intelligence is something employers always look for but the company wants to know how you would define it.

<u>Strategy</u>: Explain intelligence as it would fit best within the framework of a job.

<u>Sample answer</u>: I don't see intelligence as only a high SAT score or graduating from an Ivy League college. I consider intelligence as the ability to think on your feet and make the best decision from a variety of possibilities, utilizing a thorough analysis of the situation.

What qualities do you look for in an employer?

<u>Why this question is being asked</u>: To determine what qualities you feel are important in someone else, as this speaks to what qualities you strive to exhibit in yourself as well.

<u>Strategy</u>: Consider what qualities would be valued in the company culture and emphasize those areas.

<u>Sample answer</u>: I think the first quality I would look for is a strong work ethic. If you are not motivated to work hard and succeed, it is something that is difficult to teach. I want a team player. Not someone looking for glory for themselves, but rather one who values working together to meet goals. I want someone flexible to change as priorities can change quickly. I want someone who stays calm under pressure and can think on his or her feet.

What can you tell me about this company that nobody else can?

<u>Why this question is being asked</u>: To understand how your unique knowledge can benefit the company.

<u>Strategy</u>: As it would be impossible for you to have an actual greater understanding of the inner workings of the company than the people that work there, focus on how your perspective and experience provides you with greater insight.

<u>Sample answer</u>: Well, of course it would be impossible for me to know things that people who actually work here know. I can share that in studying the growth of the consulting side of your business, it is very similar to the growth pattern of that area of business of my last employer. If things continue to progress, I believe that you will gain 10% market share within three years.

What challenges are you looking for in a position?

<u>Why this question is being asked</u>: To determine if the challenges you are seeking are in line with the demands of the position.

<u>Strategy</u>: Consider the challenges that would be required in the position and emphasize those.

<u>Sample answer</u>: I would like to take a company with a strong product line and determine ways to cut costs while maintaining quality. I would like to improve efficiency and cut waste. I would also like to improve the customer experience and integrate more technology tools into the buying process.

Why do you think you would do well at this job?

<u>Why this question is being asked</u>: To provide you with the opportunity to sell yourself for the job.

<u>Strategy</u>: Focus on your relevant skills, experience and abilities that make you a great fit.

<u>Sample answer</u>: Given my history of meeting objectives in this field while taking on roles of progressive responsibility, I feel that I would be an excellent fit for this position.

What do you expect to be earning in five years?

<u>Why this question is being asked</u>: To make sure that your salary expectations align with those of the company.

<u>Strategy</u>: Make it clear that you are not solely driven by money but that you have a certain target in mind that you are setting as a goal for yourself.

<u>Sample answer</u>: I am not only focused on the money as I believe that the most important thing is to contribute at a significant level. It is important though to set goals, both for the company and individual ones as well. My goal is to be earning $120,000-140,000 per year within the next five years. Of course, that can vary based on the role that I am in and even dependent on market conditions.

Describe the relationship that should exist between a supervisor and those reporting to him/her.

<u>Why this question is being asked</u>: To understand both your management style as well as your ability to report to a supervisor.

<u>Strategy</u>: Describe the relationship as best you understand the

management style that exists at the company. Describe a relationship that is one of mutual respect but where the lines of command are clearly delineated.

Sample answer: The most important thing is to establish a relationship that is based on mutual respect. The subordinate has to respect the supervisor's ability to manage and the supervisor has to respect the employee. It should be a relationship where there is open communication between the parties. It is also important that each person knows their role and what is expected of them in order to meet objectives.

What is the thing that is most important to you in your job?

Why this question is being asked: To understand what your work priorities are and if those align with the needs of the company.

Strategy: Consider what are some aspects that would be essential elements to this job and focus on one of those.

Sample answer: It is hard to focus on just one thing but an environment that challenges me to do my best would be important to me on a job. I am motivated to push myself to the limits and see how hard I can work to meet objectives.

In a job, what interests you the most?

Why this question is being asked: To learn what areas of work you like to focus on and if that aligns with the position you are interviewing for.

Strategy: Consider the job and what would be aspects of that position that you can discuss.

Sample answer: The opportunity to work with co-workers to meet our goals. There is only so much that we can do while working alone and I love the ability to gather everyone's strengths so that we can work effectively together.

Are you willing to spend at least six months as a trainee?

<u>Why this question is being asked</u>: To understand if you are willing to serve in an extended apprenticeship capacity.

<u>Strategy</u>: Explain that you would be very interested in an opportunity to allow you to gain further training in order to have an excellent grasp of your role. Depending on your current seniority level, you should inquire if the trainee portion pays a depressed salary from the normal rate.

<u>Sample answer</u>: I would love the opportunity to receive top notch training and mentorship from the management team. It would be a rare opportunity to improve my knowledge of this business formally while working. I would like to know though if the pay rate would be depressed during the training period as I would not be able to take a cut from my salary to a lower rate for 6 months.

How would you describe an average day on this job?

<u>Why this question is being asked</u>: To determine if you have a good understanding of what the job will actually be like.

<u>Strategy</u>: Think back on what you have learned about the job from the job description and the interview process thus far. Paint a clear picture of the job as you understand it.

<u>Sample answer</u>: From what I understand, the job will be a balance between preparing reports and providing customer service. In the mornings, I will be expected to go through the customer service inbox and respond or forward along the messages to a co-worker that can resolve the issue. After

clearing that, I will be available to begin taking customer services calls between 10-5. In between calls, I am to download requests from supervisors as to the reports they needed created or updated. Before the close of the day, I would assign a status report on any open projects and have a brief meeting with the customer service representative that will take over my seat for the next shift.

How well defined is the job?

Why this question is being asked: To determine if you have a clear understanding of the job.

Strategy: Make it clear that you understand the requirements and objectives of the position and provide a brief summary of the job responsibilities.

Sample answer: I believe that it is very well defined. In my understanding, I would be expected to multi task in providing top notch customer service while preparing high quality reports for management.

What is important to you in a job?

Why this question is being asked: To understand what your work priorities are and if those align with the needs of the company.

Strategy: Consider what are some aspects that would be essential elements to this job and discuss some of those elements.

Sample answer: An environment that challenges me to do my best would be important to me on a job. I am motivated to push myself to the limits and see how hard I can work to meet objectives. It is also important that I can work collaboratively with a team and to do work that is meaningful.

What qualities do you find important in a co-worker?

<u>Why this question is being asked</u>: To get a sense of what type of co-worker you work best with.

<u>Strategy</u>: Consider the job you are applying for and qualities that the company would find appealing in its employees. Additionally, make it clear that you are the type of professional who can interact well with most people.

<u>Sample answer</u>: I am the type of person that can work well with any type of person. The qualities that I would prefer in a co-worker is someone that is a real team player, honest, open to suggestions and ready to work together to meet our goals.

How will this job fit in to your career plans?

<u>Why this question is being asked</u>: To understand if this job is the right fit for you.

<u>Strategy</u>: Utilize a detailed description to make the employer understand why this position would be a great fit for you.

<u>Sample answer</u>: I have worked my whole career to get to this point. I have worked my way up from coordinator and junior roles over the last 7 years to gain the required experience and build up a history of accomplishment to be qualified for this opportunity. I know that I would have the opportunity to prove myself and grow in this position.

Give me an example of a time when you had to think out of the box.

<u>Why this question is being asked</u>: To understand how you take a creative approach to problem solving.

<u>Strategy</u>: Provide an example that would be relevant to the employer of when you used a non-traditional approach to solve a problem.

<u>Sample answer</u>: It was important that I tracked down a former client. His phone number and email were no longer current. I remembered that he was an amateur chess enthusiast and joined some of the online communities in that areas to see if anyone knew him. Luckily, some people on the message boards knew him and helped to reconnect us. We were able to pitch him on an opportunity and secure the business.

What factors most influence your willingness to take a risk?

<u>Why this question is being asked</u>: To understand when and why you take risks.

<u>Strategy</u>: Provide some clarity as to your thought process in taking calculated risks.

<u>Sample answer</u>: As it is not only a risk that affects myself but my co-workers and the company as well, I have to be thoughtful about the whole process. I consider what are the reasons the risk is being taken, what are the alternative possibilities and what are the potential outcomes. If possible, I also like to confer with a respected colleague before making a final decision.

In your opinion, what are the advantages of working as a part of a team?

<u>Why this question is being asked</u>: To understand what you think about being a member of a team.

<u>Strategy</u>: Focus on the positives of working collaboratively and provide an example based on a past success that you had experienced by participating in a team.

<u>Sample answer</u>: Everyone has their own strengths and we can only achieve so much alone but by working effectively together, we achieve so much more. One project stands out to me. We were pitching a major firm to get the advertising account. We were able to brainstorm with each other and play off of each others strengths, some of us focused on the presentation aspects while others worked on research elements. We would not have achieved what we did, and secured the account, if we did not closely collaborate together.

If you found out that one of your co-workers was doing something dishonest, what would you do?

<u>Why this question is being asked</u>: To learn how you would handle a difficult situation involving a co-worker.

<u>Strategy</u>: Make it clear that you would follow the company protocol.

<u>Sample answer</u>: As I am a representative of my company, I would check with HR as to the appropriate steps to report the situation. If a co-worker was doing something dishonest, it could hurt the company overall so I would take the appropriate steps necessary to resolve it.

On a scale from 1-5 (one being the lowest) how do you rate your communication skills?

<u>Why this question is being asked</u>: To better understand your confidence in communicating as well as your ability to evaluate your own skills.

<u>Strategy</u>: Describe with confidence the steps you've taken to become a strong communicator but where there is still room for improvement.

<u>Sample answer</u>: A 4. I've made a conscious effort to improve my communication abilities. I regularly attend toastmasters meet ups to practice public speaking. I have been speaking on behalf of the company at several conferences and I've received positive feedback from attendees. In terms of the phone and email, I regularly field calls and emails from potential clients. But I think there is always room for improvement.

What are your plans for self-improvement?

<u>Why this question is being asked</u>: To learn if you plan to continue to improve yourself.

<u>Strategy</u>: Provide concrete answers as to how you will continue to learn and improve.

<u>Sample answer</u>: I am involved in several initiatives to continue to improve myself. I attend regular meetings with toastmasters to improve my public speaking abilities. I'm registered to begin a masters program in the fall and I've joined an industry mentoring program.

In your opinion, what is the difference between a vision and a mission?

<u>Why this question is being asked</u>: To determine if you understand the different in terminology related to company goals.

<u>Strategy</u>: Answer the question to your best understanding of the terminology.

<u>Sample answer</u>: A vision statement is focused on the future goals of the company. The mission statement relates to the current objectives and focus of the company.

Which of your personal characteristics do you feel enhances your effectiveness in communicating with others?

<u>Why this question is being asked</u>: To learn what unique qualities make you an effective communicator.

<u>Strategy</u>: Focus on characteristics that are relevant to you that make you a strong communicator. Provide an example that demonstrates why your characteristics were helpful.

<u>Sample answer</u>: I am patient and a good listener. Normally, when people are trying to communicate, they want to make sure that they are heard. I make sure to listen to what people have to say before responding to them. For example, I was able to secure an account by just listening to a CEO, who had seemed stressed out at a conference. He could tell that I was interested in what he had to say and I provided him with some genuine advice to resolve some of his problems. We were able to stay in touch and did business together.

What is one area in which you think you could improve your

performance?

<u>Why this question is being asked</u>: To understand what area you can improve in.

<u>Strategy</u>: Don't provide something essential to the job that you are lacking. Provide a peripheral area in which you are improving.

<u>Sample answer</u>: Well, I know for this position you would prefer someone who is bilingual. I can communicate in Spanish based on my high school and college coursework but I do need to improve. I've been practicing with Rosetta Stone software on the weekends.

Why haven't you had many interviews?

<u>Why this question is being asked</u>: To understand how proactive you have been in your job search.

<u>Strategy</u>: Make it clear that you have been focused on finding an appropriate job and not just applying to every open vacancy.

<u>Sample answer</u>: I've been applying to three or four positions a week as I am only looking to make a transition if it would be the type of opportunity that would challenge me and be a good fit at this point in my career.

How many applications have you made?

<u>Why this question is being asked</u>: To understand how proactive you have been in your job search.

<u>Strategy</u>: Make it clear that you have been focused on finding an appropriate job and not just applying to every open vacancy.

<u>Sample answer</u>: I've been applying to three or four positions a week as I am only looking to make a transition if it would be the type of opportunity that would challenge me and be a good fit at this point in my career.

If you had an opportunity to develop a basic set of values and beliefs which would serve as a company's foundation for success, what would those be?

<u>Why this question is being asked</u>: To better understand your value system.

<u>Strategy</u>: Consider the organization and what values and beliefs would be relevant to the industry.

<u>Sample answer</u>: For a business that deals with customers, the most important core value is respect of the customer. In order to have long term success as an organization, the company has to value providing the best service and product possible to meet the needs of the company.

Can you describe a situation in which you dealt with confrontation?

<u>Why this question is being asked</u>: Conflict can occur in a job situation and the interviewer would like to know how you best deal with it.

<u>Strategy</u>: Provide a situation in which a conflict was successfully resolved. Explain the situation, why conflict occurred and what the end result was.

<u>Sample answer</u>: A co-worker was taking credit for an assignment that I and my team had completed. If it was just on behalf of myself, I would have considered letting it go. I spoke to this person who claimed that he did not know what I was talking about. I asked if I could have a few moments to

explain the situation as I saw it. He said that he could understand from my perspective why it seemed like he took credit. He apologized and spoke with the CEO about the miscommunication and things were smoothed over.

What gets you out of bed in the morning?

<u>Why this question is being asked</u>: To learn what motivates you.

<u>Strategy</u>: Describe your strong work ethic and the objectives you are looking to achieve.

<u>Sample answer</u>: Besides my daughter waking me up to watch Sesame Street? But seriously, I have a very strong work ethic and I am motivated to meet whatever challenges the day has for me. I enjoy my work.

How much money do you need to make?

<u>Why this question is being asked</u>: To learn what your salary expectations are.

<u>Strategy</u>: Make it clear that you are not only focused on money. Provide a salary range as opposed to a specific number.

<u>Sample answer</u>: It's not just about the money for me as I enjoy this type of work. Based on my position in this field, I would expect to make between $80,000-100,000 per year.

What expectations do you have for your future employer?

<u>Why this question is being asked</u>: To determine if your expectations of the employer align with those of the company.

<u>Strategy</u>: Focus on the support that you would need to successfully work in a position at the company.

<u>Sample answer</u>: I expect an environment that challenges me to do my best. I would expect clear direction as to what will be required of me and how that will be measured.

What challenges are you looking for in a position?

<u>Why this question is being asked</u>: To determine how you approach challenges on a job and what challenges you may expect to face.

<u>Strategy</u>: Consider the challenges facing the industry for which you are interviewing. Focus on a couple of those challenges in providing your answer.

<u>Sample answer</u>: I am looking to face the challenge of determining the most effective way to utilize resources to remain competitive in the advertising sales market.

What is your approach to handling conflict?

<u>Why this question is being asked</u>: Conflict on a job is a common occurrence and the interviewer wants to understand how you would manage it.

<u>Strategy</u>: Describe your techniques for handling conflict and a relevant example of how you handled conflict on the job.

<u>Sample answer</u>: I believe the most important aspect to

resolving conflict is having open communication. Many sources of conflict are based on miscommunication or misunderstandings. Once you have the opportunity to talk through the issues with someone, it is easier to resolve. About two years into my first job, I reported to a new manager. The new manager's style was very different from my previous supervisor's style, and it took some time to adjust. One manager was very hands on while the other was hands off and they each preferred different means of communication and reporting information. After a few miscommunications with the new manager, I asked for a meeting to go over my expectations and clear the air. It was very helpful and we actually ended up working very well together after that.

Why are you looking for a new job?

<u>Why this question is being asked</u>: To understand the reason you are looking for a new job.

<u>Strategy</u>: Provide an explanation that focuses on why your current situation was no longer working out for you, what you learned and why a new situation would be a better fit for you in the future.

<u>Sample answer</u>: I had been at my last job for four years. It was a great experience because I was able to be with the company as we grew from a team of four to twenty employees. I was given the opportunity to train others and serve in a team leadership role. As the industry in now in a downturn, the team dwindled down and my ability to use my new skills dwindled with it. I am looking to apply my skills and experience that I have gained towards a new opportunity.

Do you feel you have strong opinions about others?

<u>Why this question is being asked</u>: To understand how/when you make judgments about other people.

<u>Strategy</u>: Explain that you feel you are a good judge of character but you are not quick to form judgments about others.

<u>Sample answer</u>: I feel that I am a good judge of character. I don't like to form early opinions of a person before I get to know them. I have an open mind and develop a professional relationship without any preconceived notions.

How would you describe yourself to a stranger at a party?

<u>Why this question is being asked</u>: To understand how you perceive yourself and want others to perceive you.

<u>Strategy</u>: You are asked in a professional context how you describe yourself in a personal situation. Focus on the professional aspects of who you are when providing your answer.

<u>Sample answer</u>: When describing the professional aspects of myself at a party, I say that I am an accountant who has specialized in the non-profit industry. I really enjoy my role in helping the organization to do good work.

Are you hoping for advancement within the company?

<u>Why this question is being asked</u>: To understand your expectations for growing your career at the company.

<u>Strategy</u>: Make it clear that you are someone who is always looking to grow and advance, but that given the opportunity you are presently serious about proving yourself in the role

available.

Sample answer: I am looking to prove myself in the role that you have available. If I prove myself, of course I am looking to advance so that I can have an even greater impact in helping the company. The title isn't as important to me as the opportunity to make a significant contribution.

Do you meet the application requirements?

Why this question is being asked: To determine if you are qualified for the job.

Strategy: Discuss the major qualifications of the job and demonstrate that you meet those.

Sample answer: Yes, I feel that I am a strong match for the requirements of the position. I have more than 10 years of experience in the accounting field, with most of it performed in the public sector. My computer skills are strong and I have a proven ability to work with multinational corporations.

What do you do to attempt to motivate your co-workers?

Why this question is being asked: Being a co-worker that can help to motivate other team members to be more productive and produce better work is always valued by employers.

Strategy: Explain the type of things that you do to motivate co-workers both proactively and by leading through example. Provide a relevant example that demonstrates your motivational techniques.

Sample answer: The first thing I do to motivate my co-workers is to maintain a positive attitude and demonstrate a strong work ethic no matter what is going on. I think my positive example in the office motivates people to work harder as well. I am also a good listener and people often tell me of the challenges and stresses of their work. I help them to gain a perspective on what they are doing and to understand why the work is not only a reflection on themselves but those around them. About once a month, I ask my co-workers to meet me in the cafeteria for lunch so that we can talk about our upcoming projects and motivate each other to push through to meet the deadlines.

How do you define teamwork?

Why this question is being asked: As teamwork is an important part of the workplace, the interviewer wants to understand what teamwork means to you.

Strategy: Provide some clarity as to how you define teamwork.

Sample answer: Teamwork means that a group of people put ego to the side and work together to meet our objectives for mutual success.

What do you do to help those unfamiliar with technology understand it better?

Why this question is being asked: As technology is a tool of ever increasing importance in the workplace, the interviewer would like to understand how you can help clients or co-workers to have a better grasp of technology.

Strategy: Explain the process you would take in helping to assist others. If available, provide a relevant example of the steps you took to help someone grasp technology better in the past.

Sample answer: I think it is important to demonstrate

through example and provide a tip sheet or step by step directions that help people to better grasp the material. I have helped both co-workers and clients to better understand technology. For example, one of our clients wanted to understand how to use LinkedIn better. I prepared some screenshots with step by step directions below the images. We reviewed it together and then I watched while the client attempted to use it herself. I was there to help correct and provide suggestions. After a couple of sessions, she felt much more comfortable using the website.

Have you ever postponed a decision? Why?

<u>Why this question is being asked</u>: The ability to make decisions is an important trait of an employee with management potential.

<u>Strategy</u>: Provide an example of when you had to postpone a decision and why it ended up working out for the best.

<u>Sample answer</u>: Before the close of the 2013 fiscal year, our company was entertaining two bids to provide management services for our company. Both were excellent firms but were pressuring us to sign a deal before the close of the year so that their fiscal number would look stronger. I decided to postpone deciding who we were picking before the end of the year as the market looked uncertain and I felt that we could get a more competitive bid after the new year. It was a risk as we could have lost both accounts or the bid could have gone up. It worked out for the better as the market got soft and we were able to secure a better deal from one of the companies in January.

If you were CEO of this company, what would you change?

<u>Why this question is being asked</u>: To ascertain your understanding of the business and suggestions for improvement.

<u>Strategy</u>: Be cautious about providing too ambitious an answer so that you don't appear to be a "know it all". However, the interviewer does want an answer. Consider what changes the industry is undergoing at the moment and provide a suggestion that is relevant to trends in the field.

<u>Sample answer</u>: As I have not sat in the CEO's chair before, I would not want to claim that I have an easy answer given today's difficult job market. From what I understand, many firms in this industry are converting to a technology based model and utilizing social media as an effective marketing tool. I feel that some resources can be shifted from the cold calling model towards this technology based model, and towards making customer experience with the technology model more interactive.

What are your pet peeves?

<u>Why this question is being asked</u>: To determine how you would fit into the company culture.

<u>Strategy</u>: Focus on annoying traits that are negatives on the job.

<u>Sample answer</u>: Most things don't bother me, but my pet peeves are laziness and lying. For me to work effectively in a team, we all have to work hard and be upfront about what is going on.

How would you define good customer service?

<u>Why this question is being asked</u>: As excellent customer

service skills are an essential aspect to many jobs, the interviewer would like to know what it means to you.

Strategy: Provide a thoughtful definition and give a relevant example.

Sample answer: Good customer service is going the extra mile to help the customer to solve his/her problem. If the customer is taking the time to reach out to you, you should be doing all you can to help. While managing a call center, one of our reps. got a call that our product had just broken but was two weeks out of warranty. I authorized a replacement as this was a loyal customer who then praised our company and thanked us on Twitter.

What quality of yours matters the most in your career?

Why this question is being asked: To determine what quality you have that would make you stand out as an employee.

Strategy: Discuss a quality that would be valued by the employer. Provide a relevant example that occurred on the job.

Sample answer: The most important quality to me is my work ethic. Once I have a job to do, I am very determined to complete it. For example, we were able to secure a major account a week before Thanksgiving. Our client understood that the holidays were right around the corner and did not expect our initial draft until late January. I thought it was important to provide quality work as early as possible to get off on the right foot. I worked through the holidays and our client had the draft by January 2nd.

Do you need additional training?

<u>Why this question is being asked</u>: To determine how much additional training you will need to do the job effectively.

<u>Strategy</u>: If you will require extensive training, make it clear to the interviewer that you are a quick learner and can take on much of the self directed learning on your off hours. If you are experienced in the field and job-ready, explain that you will require little training beyond the policies and procedures of the company as well as internal systems.

<u>Sample answer</u>: I've been working in this field for several years so I don't think I'll require an extensive amount of training. I would need to make sure I am on the same page with the company in terms of your policies and procedures as well as learn your database and sales tracking tools.

How do you feel about being on call?

<u>Why this question is being asked</u>: If you are ready to make yourself available during off hours and for unexpected situations.

<u>Strategy</u>: If this is the nature of the business (such as in technology management), let the interviewer know that you are aware that being on call is required and you will be available.

<u>Sample answer</u>: In this field, I know that having someone available to provide support in unexpected situations is a necessity so I have no problem with being on call.

What are your expectations regarding promotions?

<u>Why this question is being asked</u>: To determine your expectations in terms of career growth and how those align with the expectations of the company.

<u>Strategy</u>: Make it clear that the specific title is not as important to you as the ability to continue to grow and take on additional responsibilities.

<u>Sample answer</u>: I would like to take on additional responsibilities as I prove myself and grow in the job. The actual title is not as important to me. I would assume that once I prove myself that more opportunity will open and I'll be able to grow here.

How do you stay energized at work?

<u>Why this question is being asked</u>: To determine how much enthusiasm you bring to the workplace and how you maintain that enthusiasm.

<u>Strategy</u>: Discuss how you are naturally energetic and enthusiastic to do your best when a company puts its trust in you. Provide a relevant example of how you remained energized in a demanding situation at work.

<u>Sample answer</u>: I know that the team is counting on me to do my best while I am at work so I am naturally energized to do my best. There is always a new challenge to overcome, and that makes me enthusiastic to prove myself. For example, I once worked with my team for two weeks straight, with long nights and work on the weekends, to submit a proposal. Just as we handed it in, we heard of another similar opportunity and we were excited to jump right in and start the process all over again.

Tell me, what is the first thing you would do if you got this position?

<u>Why this question is being asked</u>: To determine if you have considered your plan of action when you get started in a new

job.

<u>Strategy</u>: Explain how you will get a sense of the company culture and best way of supporting employees by introducing yourself to your co-workers and asking how you can best support them.

<u>Sample answer</u>: I would make sure to introduce myself to my co-workers. As they have been here for years, they have a better sense of the right way of doing things and can let me know of some of the challenges that I will face.

What training do you think you will require doing this job?

<u>Why this question is being asked</u>: To determine how much additional training you will need to do the job effectively.

<u>Strategy</u>: If you will require extensive training, make it clear to the interviewer that you are a quick learner and can take on much of the self directed learning on your off hours.

If you are experienced in the field and job-ready, explain that you will require little training beyond the policies and procedures of the company as well as internal systems.

<u>Sample answer</u>: I've been working in this field for several years so I don't think I'll require an extensive amount of training. I would need to make sure I am on the same page with the company in terms of your policies and procedures as well as learn your database and sales tracking tools.

How do you feel about company politics?

<u>Why this question is being asked</u>: The interviewer is trying to gauge how much your work would be affected by internal politics taking place in the organization.

<u>Strategy</u>: Discuss how you would focus on the job and not get involved.

<u>Sample answer</u>: I know that internal politics can have a negative impact on productivity so I do not get involved. I am the type of person who likes to focus on my work while I'm on the job.

How much notice are you required to give?

<u>Why this question is being asked</u>: To ascertain when you will be available to start the job.

<u>Strategy</u>: Explain that you are enthusiastic to start but that you would need to give two weeks notice and would prefer to give three weeks notice.

<u>Sample answer</u>: I would need to give two weeks notice. If possible, I would like to give three weeks so that I can help my employer during the transition period and possibly train my replacement.

How important is money to you?

<u>Why this question is being asked</u>: To learn about the type of salary you are seeking and how money factors into your career goals.

<u>Strategy</u>: Explain that money isn't the only factor but it is an important one.

<u>Sample answer</u>: There are many important aspects that I factor into my career such as doing work that is meaningful to me and challenging myself. That being said, money is a factor as well. I am seeking an opportunity that compensates me well based on the work that I want to do.

Are there any particular companies that interest you?

<u>Why this question is being asked</u>: To understand if you have a particular plan when job seeking or will just take whatever opportunity comes along.

<u>Strategy</u>: Discuss your interest in the industry relevant to this position and why this company is of interest.

<u>Sample answer</u>: Of course, this industry is of interest to me. Your company is obviously on the top of the list but I have been closely watching the work of your competitors as well. I would very much like to remain in this industry.

Define cooperation.

<u>Why this question is being asked</u>: To understand what cooperation, an important element of most jobs, means to you.

<u>Strategy</u>: Provide a definition that includes working together with co-workers towards a common goal.

<u>Sample answer</u>: Cooperation is putting ego to the side and working together to achieve a common goal.

Define quality.

<u>Why this question is being asked</u>: To learn what quality means to you and how you might apply that understanding in a workplace situation.

<u>Strategy</u>: Explain what quality means to you and provide a relevant example of when the quality of a company product

played an important part in your business success.

Sample answer: Quality means providing the best product for the customer for the highest long term gains. In my last position, I oversaw the production of our e-reading devices. Although the products would have looked the same and the difference would not have been noticeable until the device was in use for 6 months, we decided to purchase the more expensive battery for the units as it lead to a higher quality product for the consumer.

Define service.

Why this question is being asked: To learn what service means to you and how you might apply that understanding in a workplace situation.

Strategy: Define service in a work context and provide a relevant example.

Sample answer: Service is about going the extra mile for the customer to strengthen relationships, spread goodwill and increase sales. For example while managing a call center, one of our reps. got a call that our product had just broken but was two weeks out of warranty. I authorized a replacement as this was a loyal customer who then praised our company and thanked us on Twitter

Define commitment.

Why this question is being asked: To learn what commitment means to you and how you might apply that understanding in a workplace situation.

Strategy: Define commitment in a work context and provide a relevant example.

<u>Sample answer</u>: Commitment is doing whatever is necessary to get the job done and meeting your expectations. I have often stayed late or come in early to meet my commitments and reach goals.

Define discipline.

<u>Why this question is being asked</u>: To learn what discipline means to you and how you might apply that understanding in a workplace situation.

<u>Strategy</u>: Define discipline in a work context and provide a relevant example.

<u>Sample answer</u>: Discipline is the ability to complete the task at hand and block out distractions. For example, in my last job there were rumors that the company was going to be sold and that the new owners would have mass layoffs. Many employees were not disciplined enough to focus on the job. I put those distractions out of my mind and focused on the job.

Define dedication.

<u>Why this question is being asked</u>: To learn what dedication means to you and how you might apply that understanding in the context of the workplace.

<u>Strategy</u>: Define dedication in a work context and provide a relevant example.

<u>Sample answer</u>: Dedication is the need to do your best on the job or in a given situation. When someone is counting on me, I am always dedicated to do my best.

Define integrity.

<u>Why this question is being asked</u>: To learn what integrity means to you and how you might apply that understanding in a workplace situation.

<u>Strategy</u>: Define integrity in a work context and provide a relevant example.

<u>Sample answer</u>: Integrity is the ability to do the right thing, even when it is not the thing that is most beneficial to you. For example, there was a project that I had made a mistake on but it was not clear which of the team members was responsible. I felt that it was only right to stand up and take the blame.

How do you define empowerment?

<u>Why this question is being asked</u>: To learn what empowerment means to you and how you might apply that understanding in a workplace situation.

<u>Strategy</u>: Define empowerment in a work context and provide a relevant example.

<u>Sample answer</u>: Empowerment is having the power to take action. I feel that some of the best customer service is provided by reps. who are trusted by their supervisors and empowered to make decisions to help the customer.

How do you define arrogance?

<u>Why this question is being asked</u>: To learn what arrogance means to you and how you might apply that understanding in a workplace situation.

<u>Strategy</u>: Define arrogance in a work context and provide a relevant example.

<u>Sample answer</u>: Arrogance is thinking you are always right without taking the steps to make sure that you are correct. I feel that the best employees are confident in their abilities but not afraid to ask for help or support in making a decision or solving a problem.

How do you delegate responsibility?

<u>Why this question is being asked</u>: As a supervisor, you are expected to delegate responsibility effectively, and the company wants to understand how you would do so.

<u>Strategy</u>: Provide clear insight into the process that you take in delegating responsibility and share a relevant example.

<u>Sample answer</u>: I consider the strengths of my staff and their current responsibilities. I speak with each staff member, or a small team, about what I think they could take on and how I can support them. Once I feel that they are comfortable with the task and understand what is required, I pass it on to the project manager and provide regular check-ins and support.

What do you expect to learn from this job that you're not learning about in your current position?

<u>Why this question is being asked</u>: To understand how this job will allow you to learn and what might have been lacking in a previous opportunity.

<u>Strategy</u>: Focus on your opportunity to learn from those in the company, based on their years of experience or roles in leading a company that is uniquely positioned in the market.

<u>Sample answer</u>: My current position has been great in allowing me to learn more about this industry from the perspective of a mid-sized business with a domestic market. With this company, I would be able to learn more about international businesses from a firm with a billion dollar market cap and over 10,000 employees.

Would you say that you can easily deal with high-pressure situations?

<u>Why this question is being asked</u>: To understand how you manage pressure.

<u>Strategy</u>: Provide some insight into your process of dealing with high-pressure situations.

<u>Sample answer</u>: First I acknowledge that it is not easy to deal with a high pressure situation. I make an extensive plan to best manage that situation in order to meet objectives. I like to start early to take some of the pressure off and designate responsibilities so that the most qualified people are handling their areas of responsibility. By creating time to retool or rethink any roadblocks or mistakes, it takes some of the pressure off and I am able to do my best work.

Do you have a geographic preference?

<u>Why this question is being asked</u>: If it is an international business, there might be several opportunities available and the interviewer would like to know where you would like to be located.

<u>Strategy</u>: "Anywhere!" is a dangerous answer unless you have researched where the company has branches and are truly willing to live in any of those locations.

<u>Sample answer</u>: I am open to anywhere in North America, with a preference towards the northeast.

By providing an example, convince me that you can adapt to a wide variety of people, situations and environments.

<u>Why this question is being asked</u>: Being able to work with a diverse population is an essential part of working in many positions, especially if the company is located in a major metropolitan city.

<u>Strategy</u>: Provide a relevant example from a job that demonstrates how you successfully worked with a diverse population.

<u>Sample answer</u>: I worked for a refugee assistance program. Not only were our clients from all over the world, but my co-workers were as well! Despite coming from very different backgrounds, we worked together successfully to help those in need. We leaned on each other to get familiar with other cultures and practices in order to best understand the clients and work with them effectively.

What suggestions do you have for our organization?

<u>Why this question is being asked</u>: To understand what you think about the company now and if you have considered ways for the company to improve.

<u>Strategy</u>: Be cautious here in saying anything overly negative about the company but you do want to provide an answer that shows you've considered ways that the company could improve.

<u>Sample answer</u>: As your history of success shows, you are doing so many things right and I would like to get the experience of learning about the company before I suggest any major improvements. I would say that while your presence in traditional bookstores is strong, there could be some improvement in ebook marketing as the numbers do show that ebooks are outselling traditional books in many cases.

Describe a time when you put your needs aside to help a co-worker.

<u>Why this question is being asked</u>: To understand if you are a team player and willing to help your co-workers.

<u>Strategy</u>: Provide an example of a time you helped a co-worker and describe the situation in detail. Why did the person need assistance? What did you do to help? What was the end result?

<u>Sample answer</u>: Our marketing coordinator was promoted to a new position. A recent college graduate replaced her and seemed to be struggling to manage the work. The previous employee provided a brief training but was too busy with her new job to provide additional step-by-step directions. I asked the new employee if he wanted to order lunch in for the next week and offered to spend my lunch break with him, going

over the steps to make his job easier and making sure he did not miss anything. It was helpful as he was able to grasp the material and settled into the job.

What do you do when you are faced with an obstacle to completing an important project?

<u>Why this question is being asked</u>: As every job has various obstacles to overcome, the interviewer wants to understand your process for dealing with them.

<u>Strategy</u>: Provide a clear example of the type of obstacle you have encountered, what you did to manage it and the end result.

<u>Sample answer</u>: When faced with an obstacle, I consider all alternative paths to achieve the goal as well as what type of strategy I can take to remove the obstacle. I am asked to plan our yearly conference. The most important step is to secure a venue and a date and then everything can follow after that. In reaching out to our usual venue, I was finding it difficult to secure a date as the weeks went by. I decided to seek out comparable venues, receive bids and plan all the steps that we would need to take for either venue. Once I had things set with the alternative spot, we moved forward with that venue and date and it turned out to be an even better experience.

Describe a team experience you found disappointing.

<u>Why this question is being asked</u>: Not all group experiences will be positive. The interviewer would like to know why a team experience did not work out and how you dealt with it.

<u>Strategy</u>: Provide an example relevant to the job. Explain what the situation was that necessitated teamwork, why it did not work out as expected and what you learned from it.

Sample answer: Our CEO asked every department to send a representative to serve on the recruitment committee. It was thought that the more people involved, the better. It turned out to be a mess as each person had his or her own departmental priorities and expectations for how recruitment would take place. It was hard to come to a consensus on many things and time was wasted. I learned from the situation to request that a smaller team be assembled, that those who participate want to be there and that there should be a project leader to oversee a similar initiative.

What criteria are you using to choose companies to interview with?

Why this question is being asked: To determine if you have a specific plan in seeking the next job opportunity or if you will take any job.

Strategy: Provide examples of criteria that are relevant to the job you are interviewing for. Specifically mention your interest in that industry.

Sample answer: I have been accepting interviews with Fortune 500 companies in the advertising industry. I am specifically seeking those organizations that do business overseas, support professional development and encourage teamwork.

What do you prefer: recruitment or selection?

<u>Why this question is being asked</u>: To determine if you are the type of person who likes to go out and find something or to choose from the best of what is available.

<u>Strategy</u>: Focusing on the recruitment process shows that you are proactive and a go getter as opposed to picking the best of what is available.

<u>Sample answer</u>: I like the recruitment process. I'd like to go out there and help find the people that you are looking for.

Which is more important: creativity or efficiency?

<u>Why this question is being asked</u>: To learn your methods in executing your work and how effective that makes you.

<u>Strategy</u>: Focus on a strategy that makes it clear that you are willing to prioritize what is most important for that given situation in order to meet company objectives.

<u>Sample answer</u>: I feel that most of the time it is efficiency. If you are not being efficient and trying to demonstrate creative energies, you are probably not doing your job most effectively. Now in certain situations, the best way to be most efficient is to be creative first so in that case, creativity would be prioritized.

What, in your opinion, are the key ingredients in guiding and maintaining successful business relationships?

<u>Why this question is being asked</u>: To understand your strategy for maintaining accounts and managing relationships

<u>Strategy</u>: Provide clear insight into your strategy and provide an example relevant to the job.

Sample answer: I believe the key priorities are to put the other person's needs first and to always be truthful. By never giving the client anything to worry about, you are able to build trust and establish a firm ground. For example, we had a client who asked us to follow up with their former clients who had not ordered products in over a year. I explained that we would be glad to do that, but the company could do things more efficiently if they worked with a niche firm that specialized in that area. The CEO was impressed that we put their needs first. We ended up getting more business as a result.

What kind of person are you?

Why this question is being asked: To ascertain what type of person you see yourself as and how those traits would fit into the company culture.

Strategy: Focus on positive aspects of yourself that would fit well into the culture of the company.

Sample answer: I consider myself to be a very helpful person. I enjoy thinking about how I can be of assistance to others. I am a very positive, high energy person. I like to work together in groups but I can work independently as well. I am very driven to succeed and I don't mind working hard.

What does trust mean to you?

Why this question is being asked: Having trust in others is an important element of teamwork and the interviewer wants to hear about your understanding of trust.

Strategy: Provide a clear definition of trust that would be relevant in a workplace situation and give an example.

<u>Sample answer</u>: Trust is a willingness to take a risk on something because you believe the person is giving you accurate information, to the best of his or her knowledge. Trust is something that is earned. Trust must be built between two individuals or a team over time by being open and truthful with one another, with everyone living up to their words. My co-workers and I have built up trust with one another over the course of dealing with many challenging situations. There have been many times that we were counting on each other to meet certain objectives as we were all responsible for completing the project together.

Which one is better: mentoring or coaching?

<u>Why this question is being asked</u>: The interviewer would like to learn which management style you would employ to guide subordinates or junior level employees.

<u>Strategy</u>: Consider what you have learned about the management style of the organization and focus your answer on that. If it is unclear, explain when each style works best.

<u>Sample answer</u>: I think which style works best depends on the situation, the structure of the department and the experience of the employee. Mentoring is especially important for a junior level employee, to have someone to look up to and receive regular advice from. A professional who already has the tools for success and understands company structure would benefit most from coaching.

What concerns do you have about this job?

<u>Why this question is being asked</u>: To learn what apprehensions you may have about this position.

<u>Strategy</u>: Don't reveal any major concerns here. Perhaps focus on something minor related to the position that would not seem like a major sticking point to the interviewer.

<u>Sample answer</u>: The job was listed as a "funded" position. How long is the position expected to be funded for and what are the factors necessary for a renewal?

What do you see as your primary qualifications for this job?

<u>Why this question is being asked</u>: To determine if you are qualified for the job.

<u>Strategy</u>: Discuss the major qualifications of the job and demonstrate that you have met those.

<u>Sample answer</u>: I have more than 10 years of experience in the accounting field, with most of it performed in the public sector. My computer skills are strong and I have a proven ability to work with multinational corporations

How much job security do you expect in this position?

<u>Why this question is being asked</u>: To learn how comfortable you plan to get in this position, and what your expectations are regarding the type of performance necessary to keep the job.

<u>Strategy</u>: Make it clear that you know you have to prove yourself to retain the job.

<u>Sample answer</u>: I don't expect any, beyond perhaps a short

period where I would acclimate to the culture and learn all of the processes necessary to succeed on the job. I know that I will have to prove myself to stay here. I welcome that challenge as I am always motivated to prove that I am an asset to the company.

What is the next step in your career?

<u>Why this question is being asked</u>: To learn your plan for career growth and to determine how that relates to the job.

<u>Strategy</u>: Focus on the job and why it is the right fit for your career now.

<u>Sample answer</u>: I have worked my way up to compete for a senior marketing executive position. I began as a marketing coordinator, grew to a junior marketing rep. and lastly to an account manager. I think this is the next great step for me and I'd look forward to growing in an opportunity like this.

If your job was suddenly eliminated, what kinds of work do you feel prepared to do?

<u>Why this question is being asked</u>: To understand if you've created a contingency plan for your career and how you perceive your fit in today's market.

<u>Strategy</u>: Express confidence in yourself. Answer that you would focus 100% of your energies in obtaining a job at the next level in your career.

<u>Sample answer</u>: I would be prepared to step into a role similar to the one I have, as I have proven myself to be very capable in this function over the last seven years. Additionally, it would be an important time for me to focus all of my energy on securing a job that is of a more senior capacity as I know

that I am ready for that.

What systems would you put in place to enable employees to give management feedback?

<u>Why this question is being asked</u>: To understand if you can implement better processes than what is in place already.

<u>Strategy</u>: Consider what processes are in place already or if you do not know, ask. Provide a few suggestions for improvement.

<u>Sample answer</u>: The first thing is to establish a culture where employees can feel comfortable giving regular feedback and know that it will be valued. Different people feel comfortable giving feedback in different ways so it is helpful to have various channels such as quarterly employee town hall meetings, an open door policy with management and encouragement to email suggestions.

What type of atmosphere do you like working in best, one that is more formal or casual in nature?

<u>Why this question is being asked</u>: To ascertain if the type of atmosphere you thrive in is a fit for company culture.

<u>Strategy</u>: Consider the current company culture and focus your answer on what would be an appropriate fit. If it is unclear, provide an answer that satisfies both.

<u>Sample answer</u>: I think a formal structure is important as I like to know precisely what is expected of me, when I need to report to superiors, and who I will be reporting to. But being able to interact with other employees more casually is important too. In my last job, I was not afraid to reach out to the C-suite executives with suggestions as it was a more

casual environment and my supervisor did not mind.

How does a person progress in your field?

<u>Why this question is being asked</u>: To determine if you have an understanding of the field and hierarchical structure.

<u>Strategy</u>: Demonstrate your knowledge of how someone advances in the field and the steps you are taking to put yourself in a position for continued growth.

<u>Sample answer</u>: In this field, you start as a junior coordinator, move up to account manager and then to senior account manager. To advance myself further, I would have to establish more accounts with clients and show a track record of training account managers who thrive in the business before I would be considered for a vice president role. I look forward to that challenge.

Briefly describe the type of career opportunity you are seeking.

<u>Why this question is being asked</u>: To determine if the job you are interviewing for is a match with your career goals.

<u>Strategy</u>: Focus on responsibilities and opportunities that are relevant to the job you are interviewing for.

<u>Sample answer</u>: I am seeking an opportunity where I can serve as a team leader in managing client accounts. I would like to be responsible for reporting outcomes to management. I want to help develop strategies to move a company forward.

When can you start to work if hired?

<u>Why this question is being asked</u>: To determine when you are available to begin work.

<u>Strategy</u>: If you are not working and can begin immediately, provide Monday as your answer. If you are working, show that you are professional and will give at least two weeks notice.

<u>Sample answer</u>: I would have to give two weeks notice to my current employer but I would prefer to give three weeks notice to aid in the transition, if possible.

What are some of your expectations of your future employer?

<u>Why this question is being asked</u>: To understand if your expectations of what the employer will provide are in line with those of the company.

<u>Strategy</u>: Demonstrate that you are a self starter and can make any situation work. Focus on some of the basic areas of support you are seeking.

<u>Sample answer</u>: I can really make any situation work so I don't have a large list of expectations of my employer. I would expect an environment in which I am challenged, rewarded for my accomplishments and provided with a team in which we can all work together to meet objectives.

Please list an area you feel has room for improvement at the company.

<u>Why this question is being asked</u>: To determine if you have considered ways that the company can improve.

<u>Strategy</u>: Don't focus on something overly critical about the

company. Choose an area that is working but could use some improvement.

Sample answer: The phone customer service support that you provide is excellent as it seems like each customer service rep. is empowered to do their best to help. Unfortunately, not everyone has the time to stay on the phone. An option for customer service chat over the computer would be very helpful in saving customers' time.

What significant trend do you see in our industry?

Why this question is being asked: To understand if you have your fingers on the pulse of the industry.

Strategy: Review industry trade publications and websites and focus on an emerging trend that is relevant to the business.

Sample answer: The transition from traditionally printed books to ebooks will be a trend that will continue to impact textbook publishers. The price points of an e-textbook are something that will have to be examined.

How would you tackle the first 90 days at this job?

Why this question is being asked: To determine how you would effectively utilize your first 90 days on the job.

Strategy: Make it clear that you are going to be contributing significantly from the start and how you plan to learn from others.

Sample answer: I plan to hit the ground running. I know that I will be expected to contribute immediately. I plan to learn all I can and to learn as I go. When opportunity allows, I will ask to meet with co-workers and learn what has worked successfully in the past and how a person in my role can best contribute and be effective.

Do you set goals for yourself?

<u>Why this question is being asked</u>: In order to determine to what extent you are goal oriented.

<u>Strategy</u>: Answer affirmatively and provide an example that would be relevant to the job.

<u>Sample answer</u>: Yes, I believe that goal setting is very important. For example, I set a goal of making 50 sales last year. In keeping my eye on the goal, I realized that I was 5 sales shy with a month to go. I put all of my resources into hitting that target.

Will you take a drug test as a condition of employment?

<u>Why this question is being asked</u>: To understand if you will be compliant with the rules of the company.

<u>Strategy</u>: Unless there is some reason that you can't, answer in the affirmative.

<u>Sample answer</u>: Yes, that is no problem.

What specifically do you do to set an example for your fellow employees?

<u>Why this question is being asked</u>: To determine what type of influence you have over your co-workers

<u>Strategy</u>: Provide an example that would be relevant to the job. Explain what you do, why you choose to do it that way and the end result.

<u>Sample answer</u>: I demonstrate a "can-do" attitude by being open to accepting any assignment given, having a positive

attitude about it and doing whatever is necessary to get things done.

Are you looking for a permanent position at the company?

<u>Why this question is being asked</u>: If you have a history of temping, the interviewer is looking to determine why you are now seeking permanent employment.

<u>Strategy</u>: Provide a conceivable explanation as to why a permanent job is now a good fit for you.

<u>Sample answer</u>: Working as a temp was a great fit for me as a student when I needed to be able to vary the work based on my class schedule. Now that I have graduated from school, I am looking to apply my education towards a permanent position.

What would you do to deal with office gossip?

<u>Why this question is being asked</u>: To learn how you manage outside distractions in the workplace.

<u>Strategy</u>: Make it clear that you would avoid getting involved in any office gossip or allowing it to become a distraction.

<u>Sample answer</u>: I don't let gossip distract me from my work. Any place with a number of employees is susceptible to having gossipers. I do my best to avoid situations where gossip appears to be taking place, and if necessary politely excuse myself. There is a limited amount of time to get things done so I just don't have time for it.

What gives you the most satisfaction during your free time?

<u>Why this question is being asked</u>: To get a better sense of how you maintain an appropriate work/life balance.

Strategy: Focus on discussing positive activities that show you are well rounded and that you recharge your batteries so that you are ready when you return to work.

Sample answer: I love spending time with my family. I enjoy fine dining and shows but there is nothing better than seeing my daughter grow up. The downtime with my family motivates me to work harder on the job.

What may cause your priorities to change in a work environment?

Why this question is being asked: To understand why you may do something different on the job.

Strategy: Provide an example relevant to the position you are interviewing for of a situation in which you changed priorities to the benefit of the company.

Sample answer: As management priorities have changed, I've been able to modify my own priorities in the work environment to benefit our customers. For example, the operations staff had not been directly involved in answering customer questions on the sales floor. With the new manager's approval, I was able to get involved in providing direct customer service.

What would you do to drive additional sales?

Why this question is being asked: To learn what strategies you have to increase sales.

Strategy: Provide a concrete example of how sales can be improved.

Sample answer: I would teach the sales team how to utilize LinkedIn more effectively for conducting prospect research. By understanding the backgrounds and needs of customers, salespeople would be able to create a more effective sales pitch.

What do you hope to gain from working for our company?

<u>Why this question is being asked</u>: To understand if your goals and expectations meet those of the company.

<u>Strategy</u>: Focus on what you hope to gain that would be mutually beneficial to the company as well as yourself.

<u>Sample answer</u>: I hope to prove myself after being given the opportunity to lead a sales unit. I will gain the knowledge needed to effectively train and lead a team in order to meet objectives.

How do you incorporate fun into your day?

<u>Why this question is being asked</u>: To understand how you manage your day and find ways to enjoy it even when you may be under some stress at work.
<u>Strategy</u>: Provide examples that would be professionally appropriate to demonstrate strategies that you use to enjoy your day.
<u>Sample answer</u>: Well, thankfully I enjoy my work. So while I do not think of it as "fun", I do gain a lot of satisfaction. I like to leave the aspects of the job that I enjoy the most for the end of the day as a reward for getting through the more challenging parts.

How ambitious are you?

<u>Why this question is being asked</u>: To determine if you are motivated to succeed.

<u>Strategy</u>: Explain that your motivation to succeed goes hand in hand with your interest in helping the company to succeed.

Sample answer: I am very ambitious. I always go into a situation aiming to learn all that I can in order to contribute to the organization and with an eye towards growing my role in order to take on increased responsibility. The most important reason that I am ambitious is that I would like to contribute significantly to helping the company succeed.

Please tell us why this role appeals to you.

Why this question is being asked: To understand if this role is a good match for you or if you are looking for just any job.

Strategy: Make it clear why this specific position is appealing to you.

Sample answer: This job would be a great fit for me. Given your organization's position as a leader in technology innovation, it would be a great place for me to apply my skills and to learn. The specific role matches my past experience but would allow me to take on greater responsibility as well.

What do you do when you realize you've made a mistake?

Why this question is being asked: Not everything will go your way all of the time and the interviewer would like to understand how you will handle it when things don't go right.

Strategy: Acknowledge the question. Provide an example of a mistake you have made that is relevant to the job and what you may have learned from it.

Sample answer: I am not the type of person who focuses on things like regret as we all make mistakes. It is important to acknowledge those mistakes, learn from them, and then move on. One mistake that I made is not being more open to opportunities early in my career. When I was in college, I was laser-focused as to what type of job I wanted to the point that I pictured a very specific industry, role and even location. When I received a call for an interview and it was in an outer borough, I declined the interview because it wasn't exactly what I wanted. I've learned not to be so closed minded to opportunity.

Why are you interested in this vacancy?

Why this question is being asked: To understand if this role is a good match for you or if you are just looking for any job.

Strategy: Make it clear why this specific position is appealing to you.

Sample answer: This job would be a great fit for me. Given your organization's position within the industry as a leader in technology innovation, it would be a great place for me to apply my skills and to learn as well. The specific role matches my past experience but would also allow me to take on greater responsibility.

Please briefly describe why you are seeking a new position at this time.

<u>Why this question is being asked</u>: To gain clarity on your current job status.

<u>Strategy</u>: If applicable, make it clear that you are interviewing because you are seeking a position that more appropriately matches your current skills and qualifications as opposed to interviewing because you need to switch jobs.

<u>Sample answer</u>: I do enjoy my current job but I have gained a good deal of experience since I started that position and the opportunities for growth there are quite limited. I would like to apply what I've learned towards a more progressively responsible position with my next employer.

If you came across someone engaging in unethical behavior, what would you do?

<u>Why this question is being asked</u>: To understand how you would handle inappropriate behavior in the workplace.

<u>Strategy</u>: Make it clear that you would be compliant with the rules of the company in handling such issues.

<u>Sample answer</u>: Whenever I start a new job, I make sure that I am aware of the compliance rules and procedures if I were to ever face such a situation. I wouldn't want to make the decision for how to handle it only for myself when I know that the company may be counting on me to handle it a certain way.

How do you measure quality?

<u>Why this question is being asked</u>: To learn what quality means to you and how you might apply that understanding in a workplace situation.

<u>Strategy</u>: Explain what quality means to you and how the quality of a company product or service plays an important part in a successful business.

<u>Sample answer</u>: You can measure quality based on the extent to which the service that you provide to a customer leads to repeat business and good word of mouth.

If your boss gave you an unreasonable request, how would you handle it?

<u>Why this question is being asked</u>: To understand how you deal with management expectations, even when they may seem unreasonable.

<u>Strategy</u>: Make it clear that you are always willing to work with your manager to achieve a positive resolution. Discuss how you would have a conversation to further clarify the supervisor's goals, why you may feel it would be unreasonable to meet those with your current resources and what you could do to achieve the results.

<u>Sample answer</u>: As a subordinate, I would always give the benefit of the doubt that my supervisor has an understanding of what is needed to meet the objectives and feels that I can do it. I may ask for clarity as to what is expected and explain why given my current resources it may be difficult. I would likely make suggestions as to how we could achieve those objectives with greater resources, such as shifting my priorities or bringing aboard some additional co-workers to help with the project. At the end of the day, I would do my

best to meet the objectives.

Please let us know the differences of your previous job description and our company job description.

<u>Why this question is being asked</u>:   To learn how much relevant experience you may already have for the position.

<u>Strategy</u>: Provide examples that demonstrate you have already performed many of responsibilities of the job you are interviewing for in your previous job.

<u>Sample answer</u>: They are quite similar, except with this job I'd be able to mentor more junior employees and take on more direct reporting to the senior executives. The responsibilities I had in my previous job are very similar to those for this position, such as overseeing the accounts receivable process including maintaining the database, making and preparing for follow-up phone calls, and drafting letters.

What is your greatest talent as an employee that distinguishes you from others?

<u>Why this question is being asked</u>:   To learn what skills/talents you would bring to the table that would help the company to succeed.

<u>Strategy</u>: Unless you have a unique, measurable hard skill, focus on a soft skill that makes it clear you would be an asset.

<u>Sample answer</u>: I have a very strong work ethic. While some people are motivated because a boss tells them to do something or they are afraid of losing their job, I am motivated by a personal drive to do my best. I take a lot of pride in my work and I don't stop until I meet my goals.

What days and hours are you available to work?

<u>Why this question is being asked</u>: To determine if you are available to work the hours of the job.

<u>Strategy</u>: Unless it has been made clear that the job is during off hours, make it clear that you can work traditional hours but that you can also work overtime or other non-traditional hours when necessary.

<u>Sample answer</u>: I am available when you need me. I know that the traditional "9-5" no longer exists, so I plan to come in early and stay late when needed. If I am needed on occasion on the weekends, I can work that out as well.

Provide an example of a quality that allowed you to solve a problem.

<u>Why this question is being asked</u>: To determine how you can overcome a challenge.

<u>Strategy</u>: Use an example of a quality which has helped you overcome a job-relevant challenge.

<u>Sample answer</u>: One of my strongest qualities is my work ethic. We were asked to close out the budget on December 31. Unfortunately, the key data to run the report was not available until December 30. Instead of using that as an excuse I worked several extra hours, nearly up until the ball dropped, to make the deadline and get it done.

How will you manage to come in on time to the office?

<u>Why this question is being asked</u>: To determine your plan for showing up on time.

<u>Strategy</u>: Make it clear that you have a plan for making it into the office on time and provide an example of how you have done so in the past.

<u>Sample answer</u>: I think being on time, or really being early, is essential when a team is counting on you. I usually leave an extra 45 minutes to get to work as anything usually can, and does, go wrong during the morning commute. In my last job, I commuted an hour every morning and I had a stellar on time attendance record.

Can you recall a time when you were less than pleased with your performance?

<u>Why this question is being asked</u>: To understand if you can critically evaluate your own work.

<u>Strategy</u>: Don't claim to be perfect. Provide an example of a report or work based situation that could have been improved.

<u>Sample answer</u>: I have been presenting to clients on industry projections for the next 10 years. In my first presentation, I thought the data was strong but the presentation could have been more compelling. I took a more creative approach the next time and it was easier to engage the audience.

What do you think is most important when dealing with your customer?

<u>Why this question is being asked</u>: To understand your approach to customer service.

<u>Strategy</u>: Provide an example of how you are customer-focused and what you consider essential in working with them.

<u>Sample answer</u>: It is most important to make it clear that you care about what customers have to say and will take a serious approach to providing the best service possible. For example,

a customer had been very upset because the tablets he had ordered for a trade show had not arrived to his specifications and he was planning on bringing them when he came to an expo in New York. I reached out within the company and found a vendor in New Jersey who could meet the specifications in time and deliver them to New York.

What is the thing you hate most in life?

Why this question is being asked: To understand what you do not want to do or makes you take a negative outlook.

Strategy: Don't focus on something too negative, even when you are asked about something that you "hate".

Sample answer: I normally don't focus on too many negatives but from a work context, I would say that I hate lazy people. I have a very strong work ethic and it is frustrating to find someone who is not doing his or her best.

How do you spend your day?

Why this question is being asked: To determine how you manage your time on the job.

Strategy: Provide some clarity as to how you best manage your time.

Sample answer: I leave myself plenty of extra time to get to work in the morning so that I have a buffer in case the commute is running long but especially so that I can get a head start on the day. In the mornings, I clear out my inbox, check my messages and review my planner. I send out any necessary follow up emails and make calls. As the day progresses, I meet with clients and perform some of the data work. If possible, I go out for lunch to recharge my batteries.

After lunch, I meet with clients. By 4, I make sure to enter the necessary data into the system and respond to any emails or calls I may have missed during appointments.

Give me an example of when you worked with little or no supervision.

<u>Why this question is being asked</u>: The interviewer wants to know if you can work in an environment with little or no supervision.

<u>Strategy</u>: Make it clear that you can work without supervision and provide a relevant example or two.

<u>Sample answer</u>: I can work under any management style including without supervision. Once it is clear what my objectives are and how the company wants me to execute those objectives, I can do the job. In my last position, the supervisor's priorities were pulled in many different directions and he had little time to oversee my work. As I understood what was expected of me, I was able to work without a problem.

Please give an example of when you have had to communicate information verbally in a clear and concise manner?

<u>Why this question is being asked</u>: To determine if you can be counted on to provide information to others in an effective manner.

<u>Strategy</u>: Provide a relevant example of a time on a job when you had to communicate information.

<u>Sample answer</u>: I was asked to present our updated sales and acquisition policies to our customers at a conference. Anything new produces anxiety and our clients were

concerned about the revised terms that they would have to deal with. I presented the information in a way that I felt would answer as many general questions as possible and answered as many specific questions as possible from the podium.

How can one become more punctual?

<u>Why this question is being asked</u>: To determine what your strategy is to not be late at work.

<u>Strategy</u>: Provide an answer that proves not only how one can be punctual in general but how you are the type of person that is rarely late.

<u>Sample answer</u>: I think this is a problem that anyone can resolve with proper planning. A person can create a schedule for themselves of where they have to be and when. He or she can figure out how long it will take to get to each point and build in some extra time to plan for any eventualities.

What do you do when two employees are having a conflict?

<u>Why this question is being asked</u>: To determine how you would deal with conflict in a workplace situation.

<u>Strategy</u>: Provide some clarity into how you would best manage the situation.

<u>Sample answer</u>: Assuming that it is not a physical confrontation, as in that case I would have to call security, I would have to think about my relationship to those individuals. Depending on my relationship with them, I may suggest that they calm down and take some time before sitting down privately to discuss it. If I know the situation and they appear open to it, I may volunteer to sit in on the

meeting and help to moderate and help resolve the conflict.

What sort of things do you like to delegate?

<u>Why this question is being asked</u>: To learn how you best manage your time by delegating to others.

<u>Strategy</u>: Provide an example of a relevant task that you delegate. Explain who you choose to delegate it to and why and why that is the most effective use of your time.

<u>Sample answer</u>: In considering my strengths in addition to those of my co-workers, I am a people person and I am able to build up our client base when I am meeting with prospects in the field. I normally delegate the data entry and office work to my co-workers as, after training from me, they are able to input the information quickly and accurately.

How do you see this job developing?

<u>Why this question is being asked</u>: To learn if your expectations of the position are in line with those of the company.

<u>Strategy</u>: From your research into the field and understanding of this type of job, explain how you feel that you can grow into the role and take on more responsibility.

<u>Sample answer</u>: Of course, any of my expectations would need to be in line with those of the company. As I prove myself in a customer service role with the company, I would look for more responsibility to represent the organization- such as presenting on new product lines at trade shows.

You seem not to have too much experience in [required skill]?

<u>Why this question is being asked</u>: To learn if you have the

necessary knowledge or skill based on the position requirements.

Strategy: Explain how you may not have the experience on the job (if that is the case), but how you've proven your knowledge in the past.

Sample answer: While not the project lead in implementing Ruby on Rails, I did support the project manager and I was called upon to utilize my knowledge of the program. Additionally, my final project for earning a certificate in programming, included creating a virtual model based on the program. I feel very confident that I can demonstrate more of my knowledge if given the opportunity.

What do you think is your market value?

Why this question is being asked: To determine your expectations of salary as compared to what the company would like to pay.

Strategy: Based on your prior research, provide a salary range and not just one number. Make it clear that it is not only about the salary.

Sample answer: Well, it is not only about the salary to me as I am looking to contribute and become a partner in success with your organization. I am seeking a salary within the range of $90,000-115,000 per year, depending on the benefits and incentives of course.

What decisions do you find easy to make?

Why this question is being asked: To learn more about your decision making process.

Strategy: Utilize an example that would be relevant to the job.

Sample answer: Giving more responsibility to people that have proven themselves. I believe that good people will continue to do good work and if they express an interest in taking on more responsibility, I am always happy to give that to them.

When do you plan to retire?

Why this question is being asked: To learn how long you plan to be on the job.
Strategy: Make it clear that your mind is on the job and that retirement is nowhere in sight.
Sample answer: Does anyone really retire these days? Sitting on the beach all day sounds nice but that's what vacations are for. I wouldn't be pursuing a new opportunity if retirement was anywhere in my mind. I plan to stay and grow in my new role for years to come.

How do you get the best out of people?

Why this question is being asked: To learn how you can best manage your workforce.

Strategy: Stress your ability to maximize the strength of employees, motivate them and support them to do their best.

Sample answer: I believe in leading by example. There is not something I would ask someone to do that I would not do myself.

This job has a large component of travel. How will you cope with that?

Why this question is being asked: To learn if you are cut out for a job in sales.

<u>Strategy</u>: Discuss your experience in a job that involved excessive travel and/or your interest in participating in a job like that.

<u>Sample answer</u>: I have been traveling my whole career. It is not for everybody but I enjoy it. I believe that I have mapped out the best times and ways of travel. It is exciting to see so many places and new things while representing the company.

What are the major influences that encourage you to take a job?

<u>Why this question is being asked</u>: To learn how thoughtful you have been in considering the position and how serious you would be about accepting an offer.

<u>Strategy</u>: Provide examples of the type of research you have conducted that reinforced your serious interest in the position: professionals you have spoken with and insight you have gained.

<u>Sample answer</u>: I always do my research before considering any opportunity. As you know, Bob Smith referred me for the position and I had the opportunity to ask him several pointed questions about this job. Additionally, I've read several articles about the company and it has all reinforced my interest in the job.

Have you been coached in interviewing skills?

<u>Why this question is being asked</u>: To learn if your answers sound good because of excessive preparation or because it is really you.

<u>Strategy</u>: Explain that you prepare for any situation but the answers are actually genuine and reflect who you are.

<u>Sample answer</u>: I believe that you have to be prepared for each unique situation and interviewing is certainly unique. The coaching has allowed me to put my best foot forward in providing genuine answers to you.

What do you find most attractive about this position?

<u>Why this question is being asked</u>: To learn what about the job really interests you.

<u>Strategy</u>: Focus on one element of the job and explain why this is especially appealing to you. Provide a work related example to reinforce your point.

<u>Sample answer</u>: The opportunity to work closely with the CEO is especially appealing to me. In my last position, I was counted on by the executive team to provide up to date industry data and help with strategic planning and I am glad to see that I could get involved at that level in this position.

How long would it take you to make a meaningful contribution to our firm?

<u>Why this question is being asked</u>: To determine how long it would take for you to begin contributing.

<u>Strategy</u>: Make it clear that you are ready to begin contributing at a high level right away.

<u>Sample answer</u>: As I have many years of experience in the industry, I would be ready to contribute immediately. It will take time to learn the specific company procedures and practices but I think that I could help the team right away.

Your resume suggests that you may be over-qualified for this position. What's your opinion?

<u>Why this question is being asked</u>: To determine why you are applying for a job that you appear to be overqualified for.

<u>Strategy</u>: Explain why your skills and qualifications are a good fit for this job and why you have a serious interest even though it appears to be more of a junior level position.

<u>Sample answer</u>: I think that I am a good fit for the job, neither under or overqualified. Although my last title was "Manager", it was a smaller company compared to this one.

What do you think is the most difficult thing about being a manager?

<u>Why this question is being asked</u>: To determine what challenges you have faced/anticipate facing in this role.

<u>Strategy</u>: Provide a challenge relevant to the position, how you've approached it in the past and what was the end result.

<u>Sample answer</u>: One of the most difficult challenges of being a manager is balancing the demands of executives while maximizing the effectiveness of your employees. I feel the best approach is to make sure that there is a good flow of communication between defining what the executives want as well as delivering your expectations to your team.

How do you feel about leaving the benefits of your last job to find a new job?

<u>Why this question is being asked</u>: To determine if you have fully considered the consequences of leaving your current job.

<u>Strategy</u>: Explain why you feel that this job presents a better opportunity for you and why you are willing to give up some benefits for a better potential gain.

<u>Sample answer</u>: I am glad to have learned about your extensive healthcare and retirement plan as from what I understood those aspects are comparable to this job. I would be losing the tenure that I have gained in my current job as well as some of the perks like free lunches and a healthy travel budget but I feel that the benefits of this job greatly outweigh any negatives.

How did you find out about this job?

<u>Why this question is being asked</u>: To learn if you have a passive or active interest in the job and possibly, if someone referred you.

<u>Strategy</u>: Wherever possible, it is important to demonstrate an active interest in the position.

<u>Sample answer</u>: As I have been interested in pursuing a job here for awhile, I regularly check the company website. When I found a position listed in which I would be a strong candidate, I reached out to Bob Smith in your marketing department, as we are long time colleagues. He suggested that I apply.

Do you prefer oral or written communications?

<u>Why this question is being asked</u>: To determine your comfort level in various means of communication.

<u>Strategy</u>: Make it clear that you can communicate effectively through oral or written communication. Provide an example that shows when each is more effective.

<u>Sample answer</u>: I believe that I am a good communicator and in order to be adept at communication, I have to be comfortable in utilizing either method. Sometimes one works better than the others depending on the situation. If you are going to make a major announcement or discuss an important issue with an employer or client, I feel that speaking to the person works best. If you are checking in with an employee on the road, mid conference or just for a status update, an email or even a text message may be the best course of action.

Rate your vocabulary and grammar skills for me.

<u>Why this question is being asked</u>: To learn how you would assess your communication abilities.

<u>Strategy</u>: Make it clear that you can communicate effectively for your industry without necessarily having to be a grammar expert.

<u>Sample answer</u>: I feel very comfortable with my ability to communicate based on my vocabulary and grammar skills. Anyone that would hear me communicate would feel that I am adept at presenting my ideas using correct grammar and a strong vocabulary.

What types of people need to be treated with good manners?

<u>Why this question is being asked</u>: To learn who you consider important to be treated well.

<u>Strategy</u>: Make it clear that you respect everybody as that is an essential aspect to customer service.

<u>Sample answer</u>: In my mind, everyone has to be treated with respect and with good manners. The person that seems unimportant today may be the CEO in a few years. With social media today, anyone can sing your praises or lambaste the company for poor customer service.

How do you continue learning on a daily basis?

<u>Why this question is being asked</u>: The interviewer would like to know if you are a lifelong learner. Companies want to hire people that are constantly learning and not stagnating.

<u>Strategy</u>: Provide an example of something you learned recently that is relevant to the job you are interviewing for. Explain how what you've learned is relevant to your job and what you accomplished.

<u>Sample answer</u>: If you have your eyes and ears open, you can learn something new all of the time. I learn from customers, co-workers and those in my network. I recently learned more about the importance of body language. It helped me to better identify what people are communicating with their bodies even when saying something different. This skill has been very helpful for attending business meetings and establishing new relationships.

Why is continuous improvement necessary?

<u>Why this question is being asked</u>: To understand if you understand the importance of continuing to get better.

<u>Strategy</u>: Explain that if the company does not continue to improve then it is going backwards. Provide a relevant example that proves this point.

<u>Sample answer</u>: Continuous improvement is absolutely necessary as if a company is not continuing to improve, it is stagnating and moving backwards. There are a plethora of examples of technology companies who got too comfortable in their space in the market, such as Blackberry and MySpace, who left themselves vulnerable to losing their spot.

How do you rate yourself in computer skills?

<u>Why this question is being asked:</u> As computer proficiency is an essential aspect to many roles, the interviewer would like to determine how you would rate yourself.

<u>Strategy</u>: Focus on your proficiency in utilizing the computer skills relevant to the position. Provide an example that demonstrates your expertise.

<u>Sample answer</u>: I feel that my computer skills are quite strong. I utilize Excel and Access to manage data and run reports. I've been able to grow our company visibility on social media through a popular Google+ group as well as a Facebook page.

Can you perform Internet research?

<u>Why this question is being asked</u>: To learn about your ability to conduct basic research.

<u>Strategy</u>: Explain for how long you have been conducting internet research, what methods you utilize, for what purpose

and what have been the results.

Sample answer: I am highly proficient in conducting internet research. I am efficient in sifting through vast amounts of data, finding legitimate sources and utilizing the research for finding prospective clients. I have been able to initiate many strong business relationships based on my initial research conducted on the internet.

How would you handle a client coming in to town from a foreign country?

Why this question is being asked: To learn how you can best manage relationships with international clients.

Strategy: Make it clear that you have a respect and understanding for international cultures and can devise a plan that would be appropriate.

Sample answer: When working with international clients, you have to have an understanding of culture and expectations for meetings. For example, it may be standard practice to meet clients in a setting with alcohol but some clients may not be comfortable in such an environment. Part of working with clients is not making assumptions though and sharing a potential itinerary based on your understanding of the situation and receiving feedback from the client.

What is intelligence?

Why this question is being asked: To determine what you would consider "intelligence" in a work place situation.

Strategy: Provide a definition that would resonate with the employer. Focus your answer on the ability to assess a situation and make the best decisions.

<u>Sample answer</u>: Intelligence is the ability to make a decision based on a smart assessment of the variables.

Do you prefer structured or unstructured activities?

<u>Why this question is being asked</u>: To learn what type of environment suits you best and if the structure of the company aligns with your working style.

<u>Strategy</u>: Consider the type of environment for which you are interviewing and whether that environment would seem to have a preference for structured or unstructured activities. If you are unsure, hedge your bets and prove why you can work in either environment.

<u>Sample answer</u>: I have worked in both structured and unstructured environments. As long as I have an objective and good people to work with, it can be a great experience. If I had to choose one, a structure, even a loose one, is always helpful for getting things done.

How do you think I rate as an interviewer?

<u>Why this question is being asked</u>: To throw a challenging question to the mix and allow the interviewer to "take your temperature" by seeing how things are going in the interview thus far.

<u>Strategy</u>: Explain that while the interviewer is asking challenging questions, why it has been a positive experience for you thus far.

<u>Sample answer</u>: You are certainly on the ball in asking a series of challenging questions. While responding to the questions has really forced me to think back on my whole career, it has allowed me to share why I feel that I would be a great fit for

this job.

How would you react if you knew that everyone in your department was going to let go except for one person?

<u>Why this question is being asked</u>: To learn how you would handle a difficult situation in the workplace.

<u>Strategy</u>: Explain how you are able to manage yourself and your work with limited distractions.

<u>Sample answer</u>: As I have worked a number of years already, I have experienced this situation before. I was the one that was retained. It is a difficult situation as you get close with co-workers and work closely together but I was able to manage the distractions, continue along and work effectively in the job.

Would you be willing to take a salary cut?

<u>Why this question is being asked</u>: To determine how much you prioritize the salary while considering an opportunity.

<u>Strategy</u>: Make it clear that your interest is in the opportunity, not just the salary, but the salary would play a factor and that you could not take a pay cut.

<u>Sample answer:</u> The most important thing for me is the job responsibilities and the work that I would be doing. That being said, I am looking to grow my career in all ways and salary would certainly factor into it and I would not be able to take a pay cut.

Do you think this company is ambitious and if so, why?

<u>Why this question is being asked</u>: To gain a better understanding of your perception of the company.

<u>Strategy</u>: Discuss why you feel the company is ambitious and why that goes hand in hand with your own ambitions.

<u>Sample answer:</u> I do feel that the company is ambitious. As you have moved business into the digital platform in order to grow, you have shown a tremendous amount of ambition. I would like to be here for the adventure as I am ambitious as well. I would like to help you explore new markets and take calculated risks in order to grow.

Tell me about a tricky situation for which you found a very simple solution?

<u>Why this question is being asked</u>: To learn how you can manage difficult situations.

<u>Strategy</u>: Provide an example that is relevant to the job that shows your ability to navigate difficult situations with simple solutions.

<u>Sample answer</u>: When I started a new job, my boss gave me a set of folders that required telephone verification at various intervals. Those deadlines had passed. I explained to my boss that I was a team player and willing to help whenever needed but I could not provide information that I did not know to be true. My boss understood and I was never asked again.

What steps will you take to clarify unclear information, or instructions with regard to your work?

<u>Why this question is being asked</u>: Communication is key within any organization and the interviewer would like to understand how you ensure that information is clear.

<u>Strategy</u>: Provide clear strategies that you have utilized to ensure that communication was crisp and what the end result was.

<u>Sample answer</u>: I feel that effective communication and clarity is essential to limit the chances of mistakes occurring. I have a multi-level plan in written communication- the first three lines are a synopsis of the overall reason for undertaking whatever objective it is followed by step by step instructions of how to undertake the plan. I will also provide a link to frequently asked questions in similar situations as well as a note that anyone can feel free to email me with any questions before embarking on the mission.

Is detail important to you?

<u>Why this question is being asked</u>: To understand if you are a detail oriented person.

<u>Strategy</u>: Provide an example that shows your strong attention to detail and why it is important.

<u>Sample answer</u>: Details are extremely important to me. A missing zero or two in a contract can mean the difference of a company making a significant profit or having to close.

There are thousands of possible careers. Why do you want to follow this particular career?

<u>Why this question is being asked</u>: If this career is the right fit for you or just the best option available.

<u>Strategy</u>: Explain why this career matches your strongest skill sets and assets.

<u>Sample answer</u>: I did have the opportunity to meet with a career counselor and take a few career tests, intern in various environments and take on a few roles while I graduated college. What it always came back to is that I love helping people. The field of social work really speaks to me as it allows me to make a positive impact on people's lives.

Five years ago, how would you have answered this question: "Where do you see yourself five years from now?"

<u>Why this question is being asked</u>: To determine if you have met your goals.

<u>Strategy</u>: Provide an answer that shows you are in line with meeting your goals or if not, why your goals have changed.

<u>Sample answer</u>: Five years ago, I was in the financial field and my goal was to become a vice president at that point and continue to grow. Since that time, I have transitioned into the non-profit arena and the satisfaction of my work has helped me to far exceed my goals in a way that I would not have imaged before.

If you had to turn down a request from a valued client, what would you do?

Why this question is being asked: It would be impossible to meet all of the demands of clients all of the time and the interviewer wants to know how you handle a situation where you have to say no to a request.

Strategy: Explain what you would do by providing a relevant example: what was the situation, why did you have to turn down the request and what was the end result.

Sample answer: I have encountered this situation before. As a non-profit marketing consulting firm, we sometimes work with public/private ventures. One of the executives on the private side was impressed with our work and wanted us to take on their corporate accounts as well. We had to turn it down as it did not fit our mission statement but we did provide information for another agency who we thought could do a good job.

Do you like doing things in a new way?

Why this question is being asked: To learn if you are someone that is willing to change and embrace new ideas.

Strategy: Make it clear that you are open to new ideas as long as it is the best way of doing things.

Sample answer: I am always open to hearing about new ways of doing things. When considering a new idea, you do have to consider if it will be a better or more effective move.

What are some things that you may change in the near future about your style of working?

<u>Why this question is being asked</u>: To learn if you are someone that can continue to learn from the past and improve.

<u>Strategy</u>: Demonstrate what you have learned in the past that did not work and how you will change your style to improve.

<u>Sample answer</u>: Two things that come to mind: The first is that I will be sure to delegate my work, where appropriate. I am someone that has always liked to "do it myself" and that is not the most effective way to work. Also, I will use email more effectively as a communication tool. In some ways we can be reliant upon it too much as a crutch and it is important to have conversations with people.

Do you think that technology can help to achieve better efficiency at work?

<u>Why this question is being asked</u>: To learn how you can utilize technology to work more efficiently.

<u>Strategy</u>: Explain how technology, when used correctly, can create a more effective work environment. Provide a relevant example.

<u>Sample answer</u>: Technology can certainly be used to help things run more effectively. Just like any tool, it can make things more efficient or be a distraction. Our sales team uses GotoMeeting to create a stronger bond with a potential client than a phone call and saves time and expenses by reducing travel.

What in your view makes a person likeable?

<u>Why this question is being asked</u>: To learn about what type of people you get along with.

<u>Strategy</u>: Consider the positive personality traits of people that work in this industry and focus your answers on those.

<u>Sample answer</u>: Well, I normally get along with everybody but the things that make someone likeable to me are honesty, reliability and a positive attitude.

How do you initiate a new relationship with a potential client?

<u>Why this question is being asked</u>: To determine if you can be effective in establishing business.

<u>Strategy</u>: Consider how business is normally sought and secured in the industry. Provide insight into your process for securing new business.

<u>Sample answer</u>: I know that this is a fairly closed industry so referrals are key. I would touch base with my contacts in the art world who may know this potential client and ask if he or she can introduce me over an informal business lunch. I would begin establishing a relationship and slowly gain trust in order to build up the account.

What happened the last time you were angry?

<u>Why this question is being asked</u>: The interviewer wants to learn how you manage your emotions on the job and if you can maintain you professionalism.

<u>Strategy</u>: Acknowledge the question. Do not try to maintain that you never get angry but provide a relevant example and share what you learned from it.

<u>Sample answer</u>: As a professional, I try to stay away from being angry at a co-worker or a client. Sometimes, someone may do something upsetting but I try to manage my emotions. One example does come to mind though. Early in my career, I shared a cubicle with someone in a similar capacity to me. As a worker, I tend to be all-in about my work. I am dedicated to being a professional but this person was just about the opposite. He would sign on to inappropriate websites, make personal phone calls and even fall asleep when we were asked to meet with clients. The last part was especially upsetting because his unprofessional conduct was becoming a reflection on me. Eventually, he was caught for his behavior while I was able to take on additional responsibilities and move away from my association with him.

What do you do in your spare time?

<u>Why this question is being asked</u>: The interviewer wants to know if you are a well rounded person.

<u>Strategy</u>: There is really no wrong answer here but you should avoid any controversial answers. This is not the place to discuss hunting or governmental protests.

<u>Sample answer</u>: I dedicate much of my time to my job but I find that it is important to find the time to relax as well. I enjoy spending time with my wife and daughter. We like to go to the park, see friends and go out to eat.

Who provided you with the most useful criticism you've ever received?

<u>Why this question is being asked</u>: The interviewer wants to understand how well you take constructive criticism and what you learned from it.

<u>Strategy</u>: Provide an example of criticism that someone gave you that is relevant to the job you are applying for. Make it clear what you learned from the experience.

<u>Sample answer</u>: When I was in college, I had planned to go into the live events marketing field for my career. In an interview for a summer internship, the director suggested that I consider my interest in the field as I would have to commit many evenings, weekends and travel periods to the position. In considering what I wanted from a career, I refocused my efforts towards brand marketing, and that has been a much better fit.

How do you handle a heavy workload?

<u>Why this question is being asked</u>: Many jobs have a heavy workload and the interviewer wants to understand how you manage it.

<u>Strategy</u>: Explain that you are often given more tasks than one person can easily handle but how you are able manage it successfully.

<u>Sample answer</u>: In all of my roles I was given a very heavy workload but that was ok. It gave me confidence that my supervisor felt I could handle it. It would have been overwhelming for many people but I am good at prioritizing my time. I keep track of what has to be done, when, and adjust accordingly. I build in extra time for myself, such as

shorter lunch breaks and coming in early, when I need to.

In what summer jobs have you been most interested?

<u>Why this question is being asked</u>: The interviewer wants to get a sense of your work ethic and commitment to a job even when it is only a summer job.

<u>Strategy</u>: Make it clear that you were serious about any job that you held but focus on one experience that would be relevant to the job you are applying to.

<u>Sample answer</u>: I found most summer jobs that I held to be interesting as there was always something that I could learn. The job that I did find most interesting was working for a promotions street team. We were given sponsored promotional items, like pendants or t-shirts with a company logo, to distribute at busy commuting hubs in the city. We had to plan out the most effective times to distribute, where to position ourselves and how to grab someone's attention quickly. It was the kind of experience that you couldn't learn from a marketing textbook.

How have you gone about completing a task when it was hard to comprehend the instructions?

<u>Why this question is being asked</u>: To understand how you proceed when you aren't sure about directions.

<u>Strategy</u>: Show that you are careful about understanding what is required of you and that you are not above asking for clarity or help when it is needed.

<u>Sample answer</u>: I was asked to produce the year end report that would be provided to our board of directors. It was not clear what format this was expected to be delivered. I

reviewed the directives to make sure I understood them and prepared some basic outlines so I had some visuals to show my boss. I requested a meeting and brought in my materials. I explained the assignment as I understood it and requested clarity. The boss found it helpful that I had drawn up some mockups and explained to me exactly how he wanted it done.

What gives you the most satisfaction during vacation time?

<u>Why this question is being asked</u>: To get a better sense of how you maintain an appropriate work/life balance.

<u>Strategy</u>: Discuss positive activities that show you are well rounded and that you recharge your batteries in order to be refreshed for when you return to work.

<u>Sample answer</u>: I love spending time with my family. I enjoy fine dining and shows but there is nothing better than seeing my daughter grow up. The downtime with my family motivates me to work harder on the job.

Do you think it is worth it to do things in a new way?

<u>Why this question is being asked</u>: To learn if you are someone that is willing to change and embrace new ideas.

<u>Strategy</u>: Make it clear that you are open to new ideas as long as it is balanced with the best way of doing things.

<u>Sample answer</u>: I am always open to hearing about new ways of doing things. When considering a new idea, you do have to consider if it will be a better or more effective way.

Do you think it is necessary to initiate a new relationship with a potential client, or is it best to allow the clients to find you?

<u>Why this question is being asked</u>: To determine your willingness to reach out and build new business.

<u>Strategy</u>: Building new client relationships is a key to most any business. Explain why you think it would be necessary and how you would potentially go about doing so.

<u>Sample answer</u>: Even if a company feels that it is running at full capacity and does not need to create additional business, it is still necessary to create new relationships. If you are not growing your list of contacts, your list of clients is actually shrinking due to people retiring or moving into other areas of business all of the time. I think the best way to build new relationships is through referrals by current clients.

Give me an example of how technology can help to achieve better efficiency at work?

<u>Why this question is being asked</u>: To understand if you can utilize technology to create an efficient work place.

<u>Strategy</u>: Provide a relevant example that demonstrates how you utilized technology to increase efficiency.

<u>Sample answer</u>: In my current role, I implemented the use of GoToMeeting for all sales people. Instead of having to fly out to remote locations to meet with potential business contacts, the salespeople are now able to have conference calls from their computers. It has not only saved time but money as well.

Looking back on your career plans from five years ago, do you think you have achieved what you wanted to?

<u>Why this question is being asked</u>: The interviewer would like

to know if you are the type of person that can meet goals or pivot when necessary.

Strategy: Explain what goals you had set for yourself five years ago, the extent to which you reached those goals and how you were able to change your plans when needed.

Sample answer: My goal at the time was to prove myself as a salesperson and become a top earner at Smith & Jamaica. I did prove myself as a top salesperson and it is likely I would have been considered for a promotion at Smith & Jamaica but as you know, they went out of business. I was able to adapt to the soft sales market in finance and I moved into the education sales field three years ago.

Do you think details should be left to your assistant?

Why this question is being asked: To learn if you are detail oriented or if you feel that is someone else's job.

Strategy: Explain how you are comfortable delegating authority but you prefer to be appraised of the details so that you are informed and can provide proper oversight.

Sample answer: I believe that it is a balance. If you are managing someone, you have to let him/her do their job but you also want to be aware of what is going on. I speak regularly with my assistant to learn the details and provide guidance for a strategy in order to move forward.

Please describe to me the steps you would take in performing internet research?

<u>Why this question is being asked</u>: To learn if you have basic internet search skills.

<u>Strategy</u>: Provide an example of a search that would be relevant to the job.

<u>Sample answer</u>: In order to build my list of prospective customers, I would do a google search for "steel manufacturer trade associations". This would provide me with a list of the organizations in that industry. I would then go to the websites found in the results. Once I'm on the website, I search for the organizational representatives listed- usually with their address, email and phone number.

Please describe the computer programs and software that you can use well.

<u>Why this question is being asked</u>: To learn about the computer skills that you possess.

<u>Strategy</u>: Focus on the computer skills that would be relevant for the job. Include an example that demonstrates your proficiency.

<u>Sample answer</u>: I am proficient in Microsoft Office. I am the go-to guy to polish any presentations using PowerPoint as well as for running complex reports in Excel.

What seems least attractive about this position?

<u>Why this question is being asked</u>: To determine what you like least about the job you are applying to.

<u>Strategy</u>: Focus on an area that is supplemental to the job and

not a core component of the work.

Sample answer: I read that this position is grant funded. From what I understand, the position might end after one year, no matter how much I accomplish on the job. That is definitely of concern but I am very interested in the opportunity and willing to take that risk.

This job has a large component of sales. How will you manage that?

Why this question is being asked: To determine your ability to thrive in a sales environment.

Strategy: Explain that you would embrace an opportunity that requires sales. Discuss why that is an excellent fit for you.

Sample answer: I applied for the job specifically because of the sales component. I would like to prove my ability to manage sales in addition to my data analytics responsibilities.

This job has a large component of stress. How will you cope with that?

Why this question is being asked: To learn if you can hold up under the pressures of the job.

Strategy: Explain how you best manage job related stress.

Sample answer: I understand that the job would have a lot of pressure but from what I've learned about the goals and responsibilities of the position, I think that I can handle it. I am good at recharging my batteries and de-stressing on the weekends so that I can come back to the office and face any challenge.

This job has a large component of negotiation. How will you deal with that?

<u>Why this question is being asked</u>: To learn if you can handle negotiation as an essential aspect of the job.

<u>Strategy</u>: Explain your strategy for managing negotiation as a part of your job. Provide a relevant example of how you have handled negotiation in the past.

<u>Sample answer</u>: I enjoy the art of negotiation. I believe in creating a win-win scenario in any form of negotiation. When someone sees that you are approaching the negotiation process in good faith, it is easier to build rapport and begin serious negotiations. In my last role, I was responsible for negotiating a new union contract. I was open with the union reps in showing them our books over the last five years so that they could see that we were not earning the profits that they expected and why we should look towards a 1% raise instead of their 5% demand. We ended up at a 1.5% increase.

What systems would you put in place to enable employees to give management suggestions?

<u>Why this question is being asked</u>: To understand your process for receiving employee feedback.

<u>Strategy</u>: Demonstrate that you are the type of manager who would welcome employee feedback and the systems that you would put in place. Include a few possibilities to account for various forms of feedback.

<u>Sample answer</u>: I think that employee feedback is essential as these are the people on the ground who can give you the best suggestions. Some employees are intimidated, or fear reprisal, no matter how much you say that you are open to feedback. It is important to have multiple ways to gain insight. I have an open door policy where employees can speak to me at

anytime. Employees are encouraged to email me suggestions and we have a website submission form for those that want to remain anonymous.

What is your approach to solving problems?

<u>Why this question is being asked</u>: To gain insight into how you solve problems.

<u>Strategy</u>: Explain your philosophy while providing a relevant example of a problem, what you did to solve it and what was the end result.

<u>Sample answer</u>: When my department is facing a problem that we can't easily solve, I ask colleagues from other departments to listen to our situation to provide some fresh perspective and insight. We were attempting to rebrand a consumer product but we could not come up with viable solutions. When our colleagues from a different department listened to our situation, they provided suggestions that were unique and allowed us to consider another way of thinking. It provided the spark that we needed to complete the task.

What qualities make you a good leader?

<u>Why this question is being asked</u>: To learn what qualities you have that make you fit for leadership.

<u>Strategy</u>: Provide a handful of relevant qualities and explain why those make you a good leader.

<u>Sample answer</u>: I lead by example. I wouldn't ask my team to do anything that I wouldn't do. I am resourceful. I can work within a budget and time constraints to get the job done. I am also a natural teacher. I am patient and enjoy teaching people ways to work more effectively.

Would you work holidays?

<u>Why this question is being asked</u>: To get a sense of your schedule availability and commitment to the company.

<u>Strategy</u>: If it is the type of job where business is conducted on holidays, such as retail or food services, the answer would have to be yes. If it is a job with traditional hours, make it clear that you would available in special circumstances.

<u>Sample answer</u>: I would be ready to pitch in when needed. As holidays are usually family time for me, I would like to stay on top of my work when things are busy by coming in early, working through lunch and staying late but I know during the busy season that it may not be enough time so I would come in when I was needed.

Why should we hire a person with your qualifications?

<u>Why this question is being asked</u>: To give you the opportunity to effectively sell yourself for the job and convince the company to want to hire you.

<u>Strategy</u>: Confidently reinforce your strongest qualities, experience and abilities for this job to demonstrate why you are the right fit.

<u>Sample answer</u>: I understand this industry as I've worked my way up to this role by holding progressively responsible positions for the last 15 years. I have an excellent understanding of your culture and needs and can work effectively in a team to solve your greatest challenges. I am a tireless worker who will do whatever is necessary to get the job done right, before the deadline and with minimal error.

Who else have you applied to?

<u>Why this question is being asked</u>: To learn what other opportunities you are pursuing.

<u>Strategy</u>: Make it clear that you are carefully considering other opportunities but that this company is one that interests you.

<u>Sample answer</u>: Well, I am in various stages of interviewing for similar roles within the industry. I am being careful about who I interview with as I am not just looking for a change but the right change. Your organization interests me very much.

Who have you had interviews with?

<u>Why this question is being asked</u>: To learn what other opportunities you are pursuing.

<u>Strategy</u>: Make it clear that you are carefully considering other opportunities but that this company is the one that interests you.

<u>Sample answer</u>: I am in various stages of interviewing for similar roles within the industry. I am being careful about who I interview with as I am not just looking for a change but the right change. Your organization interests me very much.

What do you feel this position should pay?

<u>Why this question is being asked</u>: To get a sense of your salary expectations for the job.

<u>Strategy</u>: Demonstrate that you have done your research into the position and build a strong argument for an effective salary range for the position.

<u>Sample answer</u>: I've been doing extensive research into salary

ranges for positions such as this in our geographic area, both from examining ranges listed in job vacancies to speaking to colleagues and even reviewing government salary databases. From what I've found, positions such as this at your sized company would pay between $70,000-$110,000. Someone with my background typically makes the upper range of $95,000-$110,000.

How did you feel handling a situation when the manager was unavailable?

<u>Why this question is being asked</u>: To learn if you are able to assume responsibility when your boss is not available to help.

<u>Strategy</u>: Explain that you felt confident handling the situation based on your training.

<u>Sample answer</u>: It felt good as I was well trained and prepared to do the job. There was a moment of uncertainty towards determining a plan of action but I considered what I thought my boss would want me to do and followed that.

Can you give me an example of your organizational skills?

<u>Why this question is being asked</u>: Organizational skills are an important part of any job and the interviewer would like to understand the system that you use.

<u>Strategy</u>: Explain your organizational process, why it works for you, and the end result.

<u>Sample answer</u>: I keep a running "to do" list. It allows me to organize my work and re-prioritize based on deadlines and urgency. It has kept me on track to finish my work on time and deliver it at a high quality.

How will you achieve success?

<u>Why this question is being asked</u>: To learn about your plans for meeting your goals.

<u>Strategy</u>: Describe your personal attributes and work ethic that guide your work in addition to discussing a specific plan for meeting objectives.

<u>Sample answer</u>: I will be successful because I have a very strong work ethic and I am determined to meet my goals. While on a job, I do an extensive amount of research into the market, form strong bonds with co-workers in order to work together, maximize my resources and work very hard to meet my objectives.

What are the consequences of building new relationships in your professional life?

<u>Why this question is being asked</u>: To determine how you manage professional relationships.

<u>Strategy</u>: Focus on the importance of continuing to build strong relationships.

<u>Sample answer</u>: You have to nurture each relationship, especially when it is new. You have to devote time to the person and see what you can do to help each other. The consequence is that it limits your time for doing other things.

Do you think it is worth building a network of contacts?

Why this question is being asked: To learn about your strategy for building new relationships.

Strategy: Explain the importance of constantly building new relationships and why it is worth the effort.

Sample answer: It is worth the effort. If you are not growing your list of contacts, your network is actually getting smaller as people retire or move on to other concerns. To even stay status quo, you need to continue to build contacts.

Give a one sentence statement about yourself.

Why this question is being asked: To learn how you describe yourself succinctly.

Strategy: Focus the sentence on your qualities, experiences and abilities that relate to the job.

Sample answer: I am a hardworking team player who possesses an expert knowledge of Sarbanes-Oxley, with ten years of experience in the accounting industry.

How are you preparing yourself to achieve your long-term goals?

Why this question is being asked: To learn how you create a plan for yourself for the future.

Strategy: Provide detailed insight into your goals and how you will go about achieving them.

Sample answer: My long term goal is to be an executive in this field. Thus far, I've worked my way up from an internship role to a junior account manager. In this position, I would like to become account manager and take on more responsibility. I am also going to school for a master's degree, and actively participating in a young professional's organization in order to network and build stronger bonds with others in the field.

7 HOW TO FOLLOW UP AFTER A JOB INTERVIEW

You took all the steps necessary to have a successful job interview. You practiced the questions and answered with confidence. You built a good rapport with the interviewer. You left the interview with confidence and are hopeful about the next steps.

When will the next steps happen? You are not sure. It is up to the employer after all and there isn't much you can do about it, right? Actually there is something you can do to improve your chances of making it to the next step. What you can do is follow up appropriately with the employer. This chapter will teach you how.

Looking for a job has often been compared to the world of dating. This is true especially when it comes to interviews and following up. Imagine that you had a very pleasant first date. The conversation flowed and there was chemistry. You might decide that it would be a good idea to send a text to your date making sure that he or she got home ok. Sounds nice. But what if you followed up that text with 3 calls asking why your text wasn't returned? Your chances of getting a second date will go from very likely to no chance.

Following up after an interview is the same way. It is not only about how well the interview went that will influence your chances of getting the job but how appropriately you follow up. There are certain unspoken rules that you must follow in order to make it to the next stage of interviewing and ultimately receive the job offer.

Over the course of the first job interview is a great time to gain clarity on the expected road ahead. When the interview is coming to its conclusion, one of your final inquiries should relate to how many rounds there are during the interview process. It would be foolish to expect a job offer after the first interview if there are 3 or 4 more people that would eventually have to interview you.

In a formal corporate settings, there are multiple rounds of interviewers. Human resources staff want to gain a better sense of your background and work skills before feeling confident in referring you to the hiring manager. The hiring manager wants to know if you have the actual skills and motivation needed to succeed as part of the team. A team member might need to know if he or she can work with you. A high ranking executive might want to meet with you before giving final approval for a higher.

Each one of the proceeding situations must be handled with sensitivity. At each round, you should request clarity as to the next steps in the process. Even if you gained clarity during the initial interview, things might have changed so you will want to make sure you are aware of the expected next step.

In addition to inquiring about the next steps in the process, ask about an expected timetable as to when you can expect to hear back if the company has interest in you. By gaining an expected time frame, you now have of structure from which to conduct effective follow up.

Without being provided with a time table as to the next steps in the process, you are just conducting guess work. You might think a company is not interested in you when you have not heard back after 3 weeks but they weren't planning to call anyone back until 6 weeks later! Following up after 3 weeks is not unreasonable but in this situation given, it would be too early.

Take the steps necessary so that your initial follow up is not required beyond thank you notes. Whoever has interviewed you at the company, whether it was an individual interview or there was a panel of multiple interviewers, should receive a note of thanks.

Ask for a business card from each interviewer. Within one day, take the time to craft and email an individual thank you note to each person. Think about his or her role at the organization. Express your sincere interest in the position while explaining how you would look forward to working with the interviewer and supporting his or her role. By taking the time to write a thank you note to each person that interviewed you, it will allow you to stand out as a serious candidate.

It is best to email a thank you note as opposed to dropping a note in the mail. The email will arrive faster, while you are still top of mind with the interviewer. A mailed note may get stuck for several days in the corporate mailroom. An emailed note also allows for a quick response from the interviewer, such as "It was nice meeting you as well." In some situations an email response could lead to a quick turnaround in the next steps of the interviewing process as you may receive a response asking for your next times of availability.

Once you have sent a thank you note, you have to give it

some time for the employer to respond to you. The time tables given during the interview are usually overly optimistic and getting a response takes longer than the time provided, in many circumstances.

There could be delays in receiving a response from the company for a variety of reasons. Other candidates were not yet available to interview. Your interviewer was out on vacation or had a medical emergency. The executive who was supposed to see you next has had other priorities than interviewing candidates. Do not sweat it as a delay in response is not necessarily a cause for major concern yet.

Keep the time table in mind before you make your next move. If you were told that you would hear back in two weeks and that time has just passed, begin planning for your next steps. You don't want to be too aggressive in following up but you do not want to appear complacent or uninterested as well. A good rule of thumb is too wait between 3 additional days and one full business week before you touch base to inquire with the company again.

Email is best as your tool for following up with the last person who interviewed you. You can respond to the email chain of your thank you note or one that confirmed the details of your interview. That will better your chances of the email not getting lost in the system.

Explain that you wanted to touch base regarding the interview that occurred three weeks ago. Reinforce your strong interest in the position and going forward to the next steps. Include specifics as this person is seeing many candidates and likely, looking to fill many positions. This is especially true if you are in the human resources stage of the interviewing process and the last person to meet with you was the recruiter.

"Thank you once again for interviewing me for the position of Budget Analyst on April 3. I am writing to touch base as to the potential next steps in the process and express my strong interest in the opportunity."

If your contact at the company wants to provide any additional detail at that point, he or she now has an easy way to do so. If the company is anticipating calling you in shortly, the person may not respond and let whomever is responsible for the next steps in following up take over at that point.

If the company has a serious interest in seeing you for the next steps but there will be a lengthy delay at this point in getting you in for an interview, you may gain some clarity. The person will likely tell you that there has been unexpected delays, that you will be called in but you will have to sit tight.

If you are not someone that will be moving on to the next steps in the interviewing process, you are unlikely to receive a direct response from the interviewer. It may have a benefit to you anyway as the company may be then motivated to mail or email you a letter of rejection. This will allow you to move on and better make use of your time.

A few words upon rejection. Maintain your calm and professionalism. There is nothing to be gained by firing off an angry email detailing the mistakes that the company made for not hiring you. In a similar vein, do not go seeking closure as to why you were not hired. It will likely be a fruitless, and frustrating, effort and your time could be used more wisely. The company will not tell you why you were not hired and in most situations, it is just a numbers game. So many candidates apply and there is only one job opening. The company does not need to justify why you were not the person hired.

Email is the easiest form of professional communication and the one with the least barriers. An initial follow up by phone may not be positively received. You never know what the interviewer is in the middle of when you interrupted his or her day with an unexpected call. Even if the company is planning to call you in for an interview, the interviewer may not be prepared to talk with you at that moment or give you any clarity. If you are the type of person that feels that they "must" call, remind the person who you are and inquire if this is a convenient time to talk.

If you do call and do not reach the person, leave a brief message explaining that you are calling to follow up after your interview that was held three weeks ago. Assume that the message will be received. Leaving more than one message is too much and could hurt your chances of getting the job.

Let us take Al for example. Al interviewed for a help desk job at a financial firm. Al felt the interview went well. So did the hiring manager. Al was so excited that when he got home, he called the hiring manager and left a message. He left another message the next morning as well as later that afternoon. Al did not get the job. He would have gotten the job but he was too aggressive.

Under no circumstances should you show up at the company unannounced to follow up on your interview. It is not a typical practice and will not be welcomed. In fact, you will be unlikely to get past security. In a similar vein, do not use any strategies to "run into" your interviewer by "coincidence such as near his or her home or somewhere that you know the person to frequent.

Advanced technology is also not a good strategy for conducting follow up. Do not attempt to tweet, Skype or text your interviewer. He or she will receive the email an/or text that you sent. That will have to be enough for the time being.

Should you send an email and leave a voice message? In most cases, one form of communication will be sufficient. If a significant amount of time has passed and you have not heard back, you can leave one voice message as well.

Be sure that you are checking your voicemail and emails carefully in the days and weeks following the interviewer. It has happened many times that the candidate assumed that the company had not gotten back to him or her yet but it was a missed email that went to the spam box or a voice message that went unheard on the phone.

Do not try to reach anyone at the company besides the contacts that were provided. It is not a good idea to reach out to the CEO asking why you have not heard back yet for the entry-level position. The one exception is when you have a contact at the company who referred you for the job. He or she may be able to follow-up with the interviewing team and find out what is the status of the job. This will help you to learn if you are still being considered for the job and when the next steps could occur.

The process for following up after an interview will play out similarly from round to round. You will send a thank you note to the person that interviewed you. You will ask for clarity as to the next steps. You will have a time table and wait to follow up until between 3 business days and a week has passed after the time given. You will email a follow up and possibly call later. Being calm and patient will yield greater results for you.

Where the process gets tricky again is during the salary negotiation phase. If you are planning to accept whatever salary is offered without taking time to think it over and or making a counter offer, the process will be simple. You'll accept the job and be given a starting date.

When you are prepared to negotiate a job offer, effective follow-up comes to the forefront once again. If you reject the initial offer and make a counter offer, the hiring manager may not be prepared to counter your offer. If he/she is open to developing a counter offer, it may have to be taken back to the team or mulled over. This is where things could get sticky and jobs lost in the process without effective follow up.

If the hiring manager needs time to counter offer, inquire as to when you should follow up if you do not hear back. Make sure that it is clear during the negotiation as well as during the follow up that you have a serious interest in the position, that this is the job that you want and that you simply just need to agree on a salary.

Ask for clarity at each round of the negotiation as to when you should follow up. A communication breakdown could lead to someone else receiving the offer for the job and accepting it.

Similarly, if you need time to mull the offer over, ask when you can let the person know by. You don't want it up in the air that you will get back to them sometime soon. In your mind, you might think that it means next week and in theirs, it might mean at the end of this week. If that information is crossed, the company may think you are no longer interested and the offer will go to someone else.

If you are ready to accept the offer, it will be better to call first as the company is waiting to hear from you. If you leave a message and do not hear back in a day or two, it is ok to send an email as well. If you don't hear back after a few days, don't start calling aggressively and leaving multiple messages. Being too anxious will set off alarm bells on the employers behalf.

8 WINNING THE SALARY NEGOTIATION

Have you ever learned that a colleague with a similar role to yours is receiving better compensation? Perhaps you were annoyed, wondering if he had a special insider connection to gain preferential treatment, if you'd been discriminated against, or if you'd made a mistake somehow. Maybe you were happy for him, and his position inspired you to think about how you can become highly compensated too. We rarely find out the real reasons behind differences in specific compensation packages, and some factors are beyond the control of the job seeker. Fortunately, the advantage of skillful salary negotiation is available to everyone and can ensure that you never undersell yourself. Using the information provided in this chapter, you will know going forward that you have leveraged your position as much as possible. More likely than not, you will become the person who scores a top-notch compensation package and makes co-workers wonder, what is her secret?

TIMING COUNTS: DELAYING THE SALARY NEGOTIATION

Every job applicant would like to know in advance if the time spent interviewing will possibly lead to an acceptable, or exciting offer. However, patience is crucial in maximizing your chances of receiving a job offer, and in creating your most powerful position for negotiating salary. If you bring up salary before the interview, you will likely create the impression that you are only interested in money. The same is true if you bring up salary during the first round of interviews. The interview is your chance to sell yourself. By revealing how much you are looking for early on, you may be eliminated based on price or receive a lower offer than the company was willing to pay. By allowing the interviewer to speak first about salary, you improve your chances of receiving an offer and put yourself in a prime position to negotiate effectively.

When you consider the perspective of the hiring company, the advantage of delaying salary negotiation becomes clear. By the time you receive the offer, the company has invested a lot of time in you as a candidate. As more people invest more time in meeting you, discussing you, and contacting your references, your value to the company grows. If the negotiation doesn't work out with you, the company will have to reinvest all that energy in another candidate, and the time spent on you is wasted. So allow the company to invest in you! You may have been vetted from hundreds of applications, met a hiring manager in HR, the manager of your department, the person who would be your direct supervisor, and possibly even a regional manager or the CEO.

Each approval strengthens your negotiation position. Can you imagine the HR manager explaining to the CEO that he turned down your counter offer because it was $5,000 higher than he had hoped to hire you for? Once you've been approved by everyone, reasonable counter-offers are best received.

Now consider your position when you bring up salary too early. The HR manager who calls to schedule an interview has invested very little in you if you appear to be an applicant with the wrong priorities or a high salary expectation. He can just return to his vetted applicant pool and replace you with a quick phone call. Similarly, he can easily drop you as a candidate after an early interview that gives the same impression.

SELLING YOURSELF

The interview is your opportunity to sell yourself as the best fit for the company and open position. While it is true that you are also trying to decide if the job, if offered, will meet your needs, you must be careful to keep a strategic perspective in all interactions. You can always turn down an offer if you decide you do not want the position. But when you focus too much on your own needs before receiving an offer, you risk disqualifying yourself from an attractive offer by coming across as disinterested.

Prior to receiving an offer, find ways to answer each interview question in a way that emphasizes how your skills, education, experience, and personality are a match for the position. Show that you know something about the company and the roles, and that you are excited about the opportunity for reasons beyond the paycheck. Do you identify with the company's mission? Are you excited about the product or services it offers? Is this a position where you can learn about an industry that you're interested in? Will this position challenge you, and allow you to use skills you are proud of? The interview process is your chance to show that you would be the type of employee who is "on board" with the company, one who stands out from the pack who watch the clock each day waiting to collect their checks and head home.

THE COUNTER-OFFER: WHAT ARE YOU WORTH?

The first step in responding to an offer is to be sure to really understand it. While it is tempting to analyze an offer based upon salary alone, you must factor in the value of employee benefits to get an accurate impression of how the offered compensation package will impact your finances and lifestyle.

Consider health and retirement benefits, education subsidy, professional development, days off, sign-on incentives, commissions, bonuses, availability of subsidized child care, or health and wellness programs. Realize that not all benefits with the same name are identical. For example, some companies offer a single health insurance plan option that includes high co-pays and employee contribution towards the premium, limited access to specialists, an annual deductible of $3000 before any benefits are paid, and which is not accepted by many local physicians. Other companies offer multiple plan choices, pay all or most of the cost of the premiums, have no copays or low copays, no annual deductibles, and are accepted by most physicians. Find out if you will have to pay union dues. To the extent the information is available, analyzing these kinds of details will give you a clearer picture of the compensation being offered.

When the offer is made, be sure to ask where you can get information about the employee benefits you would be eligible for. Thank the interviewer for the offer and express interest in the position. Do not accept the initial offer. Advise the interviewer that you'd like to discuss the offer with your family, and ask when she will need your response. At home, be sure to review any packets you are handed and to visit the company website to read about the offered benefits, and consider how they fit in to your needs.

Before returning a counter offer, do research to determine

your value in the marketplace and the company's ability to pay. Your value is based on what the company is prepared to pay a person of your competence to fill the open position. For better or for worse, this has little relation to the compensation you are receiving presently or were at your last job. If you're interviewing at a larger company, realize that they usually have organizational charts including salary ranges, giving the hiring manager/human resources professional an understanding of the minimum and maximum that can be offered for each position. And while possibly less structured, even smaller companies have a range in mind for compensating the person filling a position. Your goal is to get an offer at the top of the range. The company might try to leverage your current compensation to its advantage, presuming you'll be happy to be paid about what you are currently making. If previous salary comes up, try to shift the focus of the conversation back towards the current position and what the company can pay the best candidate. Explain that you have gained many skills since you began in your prior position, and are looking for a new role that allows you to work at a higher level. You are looking for that next step in your career, and a salary that reflects the responsibilities of the new position and your skills for handling the more senior role, or the same role at a larger company or in a more demanding market.

Real-life example of success using this strategy:

A client interviews for a position with a salary range listed of $55,000- $70,000 a year. Her current salary is $48,000 a year, but she is applying for a more senior position than the one she is leaving. After going through several rounds of interviews, she receives an initial offer of $58,000. Ignoring her current salary and noting that this offer is on the bottom of the salary range listed in the job description, she strategizes. She reinforces her seriousness in taking the job and makes it clear that salary is the only current barrier to accepting the position. When the interviewer brings up her $48,000 salary as justification for the current low-range offer, she replies, "Yes, it is correct that I am currently making less than $58,000. In order to take the next step in my career, I am looking for $70,000." She received an offer of $66,000, the higher part of the range, increasing her salary from one position to the next by 27%.

You can learn your value in the current market by looking at a few convenient resources online. First, learn the current salary range for your field. Look at the salary advertised for similar open positions on Indeed.com. Get factual salary range information via O*Net Online (www.Onetonline.org). Next, determine your position in the field. You can compare your education, skills, and experience to others' by surveying professionals in the industry via www.Linkedin.com . If you have connections, you might feel comfortable contacting them for their suggestions about salary. Be sure to check the company website for information about the position. Sometimes the salary range is listed here even if it is not stated in the job announcement. If you are applying to a non-profit, you should be researching your value in the market as a whole. Your research should include salary information for someone working in your position in the corporate world as well. Unless you are making a conscious decision to work for less because you believe in the non-profit's mission, you should use your best negotiation tactics. Even if you do believe in the mission, you can still strategically negotiate. You are worth it, and your personal commitment to the mission makes you more valuable to the company. While a non-profit may not have the same pay scale as a corporation, you should still try to negotiate a salary in the top end of the range.

Hopefully you have been able to allow the interviewer to speak first about compensation. Having done your research, you are in a great position to make a reasonable counter offer. Be clear in your counter that you are interested in the position, and the only barrier to an agreement is coming to a mutually acceptable compensation package.

In any negotiation situation, you want to create a win-win where both parties walk away happy. Choose your counter offer considering that the company will probably try to meet you somewhere in the middle. For example, if a company offers $60,000 and the salary range for the position is normally $60,000-$68,000, inquire if they can come up a bit on the offer to $70,000. The final offer will likely be somewhere between $60,000 and $70,000, but by reaching just past the top of the range you've included the highest salaries in the realm of possibility without appearing unreasonable.

If the interviewer asks you about salary without giving any specific offer first, your best move is to answer with a very large salary range. This minimizes your risk of underselling yourself or of appearing to have unrealistically high expectations. For example, you might say "I'm expecting something in the range of $45,000-$60,000, depending on offered benefits. What's most important to me is the opportunity as a whole."

If the company cannot negotiate on salary, ask about benefits.

Maybe the company can include you on its health insurance plan, begin making employer contributions to your retirement account or allow you to immediately vest in your retirement account without the usual waiting period. Perhaps you can gain some extra vacation days, be given permission to work from home once a week, or have more flexible hours.

KNOWING THE BENEFITS OF EMPLOYEE BENEFITS

When comparing offers, it is important to know what benefits are available. The difference in benefits packages can amount to thousands of dollars a year for you and in some cases provide access to great tools for improving work-life balance. Below are some benefits to look for:

1. Health Insurance: Everyone needs catastrophic coverage, since accidents and serious illness can happen to anyone. In addition, consider whether you or your family use chiropractors, counseling, addiction treatment programs, physical therapy, regular prescriptions, hearing aids, podiatrists, or fertility treatments. The range of coverage for these "extras" varies widely between plans, so if you may be using these services the value of coverage adds up quickly. Some plans cover dental cleanings as well.

2. Dental Insurance: Dental cleanings and work may be covered totally, or not at all. Look at the plan specifics to see what you'd pay for work you are likely to use. Periodontal and orthodontic treatments are considered to be more premium benefits and are less likely to be covered.

3. Vision Coverage: If you wear glasses or contacts, you can save money with this plan. Sometimes vision plans are included in health insurance or dental plans.

4. Health and Wellness Plans: Some employers pay for or make available at a discount services that will make you healthier. It may include access to a smoking cessation program, weight loss programs, or a health club membership.

5. Vacation and Sick Days: Paid, and unpaid. If relevant, consider maternity/paternity leave policies.

6. Short Term Disability and Long Term Disability Plans.

7. Commuter benefits: The employer provides free parking, or discounted rates at a nearby garage. Transit checks for use on public transportation allow your commute to be tax-free, and are sometimes paid for or subsidized by the employer.

8. Flexible hours: Flexible start and end times to put in your hours might make life easier, your commute shorter and cheaper, and your childcare costs lower.

9. Work from home: Having the option to work from home is a valuable convenience.

10. Flex Spending Accounts (FSA): Allow you to pay for childcare or uncovered medical expenses with pre-tax dollars, saving you money.

11. Childcare: Some employers offer in-house childcare which is subsidized by the company so your prices are lower or your child receives a higher quality experience. Others have agreements with nearby daycares for a discounted rate. Some even have "backup" childcare available so that you don't have to scramble when there is a school vacation or your babysitter calls out sick.

12. Miscellaneous extras: There are many creative benefits that are offered. Free coffee, lunches, snacks, dry cleaning service, life insurance, access to corporate cars or timeshares,

or allowing you to keep the frequent flier miles accumulated from work travel. While none of these benefits are to be expected, these icing on the cake perks add value to an offer beyond the salary.

TAKING A RISK

No doubt about it, there is an element of risk in negotiating. Perhaps when you don't immediately accept an offer, the position will be filled by another candidate. It is possible that the company isn't willing to pay more for a better candidate, and will not hesitate to replace you with someone who is less qualified but cheaper. Knowing your individual needs, you may decide that an initial offer is satisfactory and the risk of negotiating isn't worthwhile.

Keep in mind though, that there are many benefits to negotiating. In most cases, future raises are based upon your hiring salary. If you are hired in low, you can not expect that the company will recognize your true value and make up for it at the annual review. In a smaller company, you probably interacted directly with the company owner when you were hired, with your negotiation style or lack of assertiveness noted. If you didn't negotiate, you may be labeled as a person who is satisfied with working at a lower pay rate, and so be less likely to receive raises in the future that might normally be given to avoid employee turnover.

In almost all cases, you will want clarity on certain offer points in order to avoid an unpleasant surprise. An informal offer may not specify the exact hours you are expected to work, your specific responsibilities, when you can expect to be paid, and how vacation and sick leave are handled. Optimistically you can hope that the unspoken issues will be handled reasonably. But realistically, you want at a minimum to make sure that the basics of your potential employer's expectations for your relationship are something you can accept. This will avoid the pitfall of feeling trapped in a position.

Below are some surprises I've been told about by clients, more entertaining to read about than to experience first hand!

A client took a position working in a group home for adults with disabilities. She was surprised to learn that she was expected to work an "overnight asleep shift" in the group home every week.

A client took a job as the executive assistant to the CEO of a company, hoping to learn about the industry and company management. He didn't mind picking up dry cleaning and doing some of the CEO's personal errands. Before long though, he found himself regularly cleaning the CEO's house and picking up after his young children.

A client went on an interview to work in an unspecified entry level position at a large non-profit organization. Though she asked many questions about the role being filled in the interview, by the time it was over she knew only that the job required a driver's license and an interest in working with senior citizens. The interviewer offered her the job on the spot. When asking about the salary, the interviewer responded "You'll be able to do it if you are frugal." Unable to get specific information about the salary, responsibilities, or hours, this client declined the offer.

A client took a position at an SAT prep agency that required him to sign a "non-compete" agreement that effectively meant that he couldn't work for any other test prep agency in the area for three years after accepting this position. He was happy with the job, so he signed the agreement. Not long after, a new supervisor whom he didn't like was hired, and he was transferred to another branch that increased his commute by an hour each way. He no longer liked the job, but because of the signed non-compete agreement had to change fields in order to find a position within a reasonable distance of his home.

TIPS FOR THE UNEMPLOYED: CONFIDENCE TO NEGOTIATE LIKE YOU HAVE A JOB

It's true: Employed job seekers tend to receive better job offers than the unemployed. But is part of that based on how we act as job seekers when not working or underemployed? Though you may not have an income right now, your skills and experience maintain their value. You do not have to start at the bottom and accept any offer. Below are some suggestions to avoid allowing a period of unemployment to have a negative impact on your future.

Realize that you are in a position to negotiate. Of course you are eager to regain a steady income and to get your career back on track. But don't allow a bump in your career path to cast you down into a negative spiral. If your entry compensation to the company is set low, it will be hard to break out of that mold in the future if you want to stay with the company. If you accept a position that is a poor fit for you, either knowingly or because you were so eager to have a job, any job, that you didn't ask enough questions, you might be creating a lot of unnecessary personal stress when a better opportunity is just around the corner. A company has just selected you as the best fit for its open position. You are the new hire it wants, so negotiate with the confidence that your skills and experience are more valuable than those of the competition, even if your competitors are currently employed.

First, make sure that you understand the basic terms or the job offer before accepting. Employed new hires do not leave any grey areas in a job offer before accepting, and neither should you. Know what the company expects of you. What hours will you work? How often are you expected to travel or work nights, weekends, and holidays? Are there any extended shifts? What are your basic responsibilities, and who is your immediate supervisor? Will you be required to undergo any training or continuing education? For sales positions, look for information about what kind of client network is already set up for you, and the extent to which you are expected to make your own connections. Be especially careful if the pay is exclusively commission-based, since this might mean you are signing on to a company with a pyramid structure, where most of your income is from sales to friends and family and the only way to make a real living is to recruit others to sell to their friends and family. Also seek clarity on your compensation. Know when you can expect to be paid, how your pay is determined, what benefits are available, and when you begin receiving each benefit.

Regarding benefits, negotiate to be hired on the same terms as a person who is being hired from a position of employment. For example, companies routinely waive any "90 day waiting period" for enrollment in health benefits when hiring someone who is employed elsewhere. The use of an enrollment waiting period is commonly used to avoid a hassle for the employer, in the unusual case that a person would work very briefly for for the company, enroll in health benefits, and then be entitled to COBRA (continuing coverage of health benefits after employment has ended) with all the administrative overhead. It is reasonable to ask a company to take the small risk of an administrative hassle, should things not work out.

You might also consider asking for immediate qualification for other benefits that are delayed, such as qualifying for employer matching contributions to a retirement plan, vesting in a retirement plan, being eligible for a transit subsidy, or paid vacation days. Second, don't accept the initial offer. You can and should negotiate, even though you are unemployed. Get a sense of a reasonable salary range for the position and be prepared to counter offer. The company has selected you from an applicant pool including employed individuals as its first choice. The company recognizes you are valuable, negotiate with that in mind!

Finally, don't accept a lowball offer based on a promise that the salary might increase substantially in six, nine, or twelve months. Unless the offer is for an internship or training program, you are fully qualified for the position and deserve to be paid at a market rate from day one. Accepting the lowball offer categorizes you as willing to work at a low rate, and your salary is likely to remain depressed even when you prove your value to the company. What will you do if the salary increase doesn't come on the promised date? The company may have an excuse to delay the raise as a way to bait you to continue to work at a depressed rate. A company that will compensate you fairly will do so from the start, so be very suspicious of big promises and negotiate for reasonable compensation.

JUGGLING TWO JOB OFFERS

Picture this: You apply for jobs for months on end and hear nothing back. You wait for the day when you will finally receive a job offer that is acceptable to you. That day comes. What could possibly be wrong now? You are anticipating an offer for a job that you want even more. How do you maximize your chance of hearing back from the preferred company without ending up empty handed?

Once you have a job offer and are anticipating another, take the following steps: Respond right away to the company that already made you an offer. Let the company know that you are serious about the job but need a few days to decide. Ask if you can have some time to think about the offer and find out when must they know if you will be accepting the job.

Next, update the company from which you anticipate an offer about your current status. Speak to your interviewer and let him or her know that you've received another job offer. Make it clear that you are more interested in this position, if offered the job. Provide the date in which you must respond to the first job offer. Ask if you can get an answer from this company by that time. Hopefully your preferred employer can give you clarity by the deadline. If not, you have to decide how much risk you are willing to take. Are you willing to ask the first company for more time? It may not be taken kindly and you could lose out on the job. On the other hand, they might be willing to give you a few more days to decide. You may risk receiving an offer at all from your preferred employer if you pressure too much. If you risk losing out on both jobs, calculate how long you anticipate that it will take until you receive a similar offer.

SALARY NEGOTIATION SCRIPTS

We've all been there. You're asked a question you aren't prepared to answer, and your response begins with an uncomfortable pause or the dreaded "Uhhh...ummm..." Avoid this common pitfall by preparing answers the professional questions you are likely to be asked on an interview. Learn from the sample script below, and negotiate salary with confidence.

What did you make in your last position?
I made $47,000 per year, but now I am focusing on finding a position that takes full advantage of my education and increased experience.

What type of salary are you looking for?

It's not just about the salary for me it's about the whole opportunity. Is there a range that you have available?

Yes, we are looking to pay between 42-48K per year.

That would be within my range.

We would like to make you an offer of 46k per year.

Thank you for the offer. Can you provide me with details on employee benefits like health insurance coverage, vacation days, retirement contributions, and education incentives?

We have extensive benefits...

Great. Would it be possible to negotiate on salary? I am very interested in the position but seeking $48-53K per year.

We can offer you 52K.

Thank you. I'd like to talk it over with my family and confirm all the details. When can I let you know by?

Answer A: We'd really like to have an answer by Friday.

Ok. I will call you first thing Friday morning. I am really excited at the potential to work together.

Answer B: I'd have to speak to management about the possibility of a higher offer.

When should I follow up with you?

Answer C: We cannot give a higher salary.

1. OK. Is there flexibility on some of the benefits?

2. I understand you cannot give a higher offer initially. Can my salary be re-evaluated at 6 months once I have proven myself? If I have, at what rate can I expect my salary to increase.

You are now ready to give a more robust answer to salary related questions and earn the income that you deserve! For maximum confidence, you may want to find a friend and practice a mock interview. Now that you've learned the strategies for successfully negotiating your highest salary offer, and have reviewed the practice questions to be prepared for salary related questions you may be asked on an interview, you are prepared to go in to an interview with confidence that you will not undersell yourself.

AUTHOR'S END NOTE...

Congratulations! At this point you made it through 500 questions, reviewed strategy to prepare yourself before the interview, learned how to follow up effectively and negotiate the highest offer. This is only the beginning. Be sure to refer back to this book regularly to sharpen your interviewing technique. Good luck!

WOULD YOU BE SO KIND...

Each book review posted on Amazon allows potential readers to determine if this is the book for them. Would you be so kind as to post your candid review of this book on Amazon?

SPECIAL OFFER

As a thank you for purchasing this book, the author is offering you a free evaluation of your resume. Just email your resume to Laviemarg@Lioncubjobsearch.com and Lavie will email you back with a few tips on how you can improve the document to increase your chances for getting an interview.

ABOUT THE AUTHOR

Lavie Margolin is an author and consultant. As an author, he has written several career, job search and LinkedIn focused print and ebooks. The most well known is "Winning Answers to 500 Interview Questions", an Amazon #1 best seller in several career categories. In support of his books books, he presents on career, job search and LinkedIn related topics.

As a consultant, Lavie can help your organization manage and grow your organization's brand via LinkedIn.

Lavie is also available to serve as an industry expert for media requests relevant to job search & careers. He has been quoted in a variety of resources for his expertise including the New York Times, Wall Street Journal and Investors Business Daily.

Phone: (845) 480-2823

Email: Laviemarg@Lioncubjobsearch.com

Twitter: @Laviemarg

LinkedIn: http://www.linkedin.com/in/laviemargolin

www.ingramcontent.com/pod-product-compliance
Lightning Source LLC
Chambersburg PA
CBHW020153200326
41521CB00006B/348